SUN SHADOW MOUNTAIN

Poetry and Art Anthology

Cover design by Donald R. Anderson and Nikki Quismondo, photographs on cover, courtesy of Donald R. Anderson, Reina Hutchison, and Patricia Wellingham-Jones © 2007.

Co-publisher, Co-editor, Chief Copy Inspector, Project Coordinator, Font and Detail Specialist, Website Designer, **Donald R. Anderson**

Co-publisher, Editor-in-Chief, Layout and Design Specialist, Head of Marketing/Press Representative, Project Coordinator, **Nikki Quismondo**

Poetry Editor, Copy Editor, **Lance Wesley Hudson**

Published 2007
ISBN: 978-0-6151-4760-4
Contact Publishers:
poetsespresso@yahoo.com

Donald R. Anderson
(209) 943-2449

Nikki Quismondo
(209) 570-7917

Sun Shadow Mountain
P.O. Box 121
Farmington, CA 95230

www.SunShadowMountain.com

Manuscript produced in Stockton, California, USA.

Introduction

This anthology is composed of the generous contributions from a group of 38 poets, artists and photographers who should be acknowledged for their charitable outlook in their collaboration. The book contains an astounding banquet of poetry, prose, photography and artwork. It is a celebration of life as well as an expression of lament. The book takes the reader through a series of moods, enriched with narrative poetry that reflects the California lifestyle, and the melancholia of heartbreak and loss, all the way through to the prolific and inspirational.

Sun Shadow Mountain originated in the Spring of 2005, when a group of poets called *The Aertherials Club* at Barnes and Noble which met after a workshop based on the book *The Artist's Way* by Julia Cameron, were discussing the title for the upcoming anthology. The group wanted the title to convey a fresh inspiration for a new generation, along with showing a tribute to the beauty of life, and through a spectrum of poetry.

Writers, artists, and photographers from the California region, and abroad, such as Texas and New York, worked together to celebrate the nature of *Sun Shadow Mountain*. The contributors donated their works and the co-editors their time and works to the project. The co-editors placed the assortment of poetry, artwork, and photography into sections that suited three themes, the first, *Sun*, the second, *Shadow* and the third, *Mountain*.

The first of the three sections, *Sun*, celebrates the various characteristics associated with the sun, such as the images and tales it conjures up and its significant effects it bestows upon the world, but in a metaphorical sense. Ideas for showing the sun in its many forms were presented through out the book. The section includes poetry that projects a cheerful and light hearted disposition, as well as a mixture of narratives that are reflective, nostalgic, and display characteristic of the sun's energy and vitality, such as in Joe Tetro's "WE'RE ALL SUNDOWNERS": *"I'll hear my grandma telling / about times of drought / when grasshoppers came in clouds / and blotted out the sun, and chickens / went to roost at noon. / And, just minutes later, / how the sun came out again, / .... / the awesome turning of energy / into heat, and heat back to dust— / .... / each of us—in his, or her, turn— / will someday follow the sun."*

The nature of the sun is unpredictable, and even wild. The poetry in the chapter shows a variety of those effects. There are poems that are rich in imagery displaying California's warm summer spirit and its beautiful landscapes. The section is a mixture of fiery and imaginative events, alongside with beautifully illustrated art work and photography that shows this focus.

The sun brings out the passion of exploratory wonder, entertaining spontaneity, and an insatiable hunger. Once thought to be the center of the celestial universe, it is still the source of a magical light. The sun portrays a duality, of innocence, and the dangerous, powerful, discomforting fire. Also it is commonly associated with the daily routines, and of new beginnings. The book showcases the sun's perseverance, and places lively life stories encapsulated in a day.

The second of the three sections, *Shadow*, delves into the various characteristics associated with shadows as imagery and as a metaphor. The seduction of the shadows induces fantasies, profound depths of one's own shadows, ethereal dreams and sensual evocations of the night's alluring escape. The shadows transition from the fleeting flights of fancy to the development of natural roots. In reading the poetry in this chapter, one can picture shadows traversing the various landscapes across the earth, reflecting on ourselves in its soft fearful hidden inhibitions. The shadow poetry and illustrations show very introspective and deep subjects, such as death and war, the metaphysical, the emotional and dramatic, and even the wickedly humorous, as in the poetry noir, such as in Stephen Wilson's Haiku, *"Wendy's stitching ripped / Pan chases his shadow / On bleeding feet."* New mysteries can always be uncovered in the retreats of the shadow pieces.

The third and final section of the book, *Mountain*, celebrates the various characteristics associated with the mountain, as imagery and as a metaphor. In some of the poetry the mountain represents a quest, to reach that exhilarating far off peak. Mountain themes might focus on nature, as in "Mountain Summer" by Gail Lee White: *"For a frozen moment she watched us/ Then flew over the rail fence/ As the fauns scooted under/ Instantly they disappeared in the under growth / It lasted only a few seconds/ But the sight was forever printed on my mind's eye."* Through portrayal of the majestic, they tribute the mountain's sense of the immortality, immeasurable scale, or timeless beauty, and inspire through the awe of the wildness which inhabits them. Also mountains in this book have been used to represent enlightenment, wisdom, as well as realizations of the spiritual sort, and truth, as in Shonda Renée's "A Poem for Sula:" *"I pour through her pages again/and beg pardon my past judgment.//She is now Eve,/biting into the world and saying,/ 'Here baby, taste this.' "*

Mountains are monuments of immovable mass, and thus represent in the poetry and art, the important things such as many issues of social and political injustice introduced by the philosophical provocative image of the mountain. The solid rock of the mountain is a metaphor for strength, power, foundations, big impressions, grand processes at work and ambition. The sheer prominence draws out crusades, determination, and perseverance. It's age is ancient and represents the tribal and ritualistic, a persuasive deity of renewal.

The structure of the book is like the journey of a beam of light towards the mountain and continuing onward. Many pieces actually interacted like characters in a play. The poems are the voices of the new generation of budding creative artists and seasoned veterans. *Sun Shadow Mountain* is full of stories, rich in imagery, spanning the various paces of life, shown in an array of backgrounds, with illustrations and photography work from a variety of talented artisans.

Acknowledgments

We would like to truly thank the numerous people who, during the many months of our journey, have supported us and helped us make *Sun Shadow Mountain* a reality, especially Wayne Robinson and Marie J. Ross. A great acknowledgment goes out to our contributors who have entrusted us with their creative works; their encouragement and patience during the editing and review process is deeply appreciated.

We would like to show our gratitude to all of the people who have established interest in our book and who have devoted their time and effort assisting us with seeing this project through, particularly, our copy editor, Lance Wesley Hudson, who has assisted in the submission process, as well as helping our contributors meet the guidelines and deadlines. We would like to thank Paula Sheil, San Joaquin Delta College's faculty advisor for the Writers' Guild, who has generously given us her invaluable insights and technical knowledge to publishing. We would also like to acknowledge Joe Clary and Steffani Migliori for their recommendations on book signing events and promotions. We would also like to express our thanks to Jeremy Outman for his input on the cover design and Reina Hutchison from *Artifact*, whose photography work, is on the cover.

We would like to commend the poetry communities from Stockton, Lodi and Sacramento California, who have given us their encouragement and support, especially, David Humphreys of *Poet's Corner Press*, Stephen M. Wilson from *Poet's Corner Presents*, Roger E. Naylor of *The Fig Leaf Monthly*, Kathy Kieth, of *Rattlesnake Press*, John Morearty of *Connections*, Shonda Renée from *Poets on the Roof*, Alan Satow, Jean Claude Crhi, Mable "Jimi" Choice, Elizabeth Parrish, Patricia Mayorga, Sergio Navarro, Patricia Wellingham-Jones of *PWJ Publishing*, Monika Rose, from *Manzanita*, Jerianne of *ZineWorld*, Mary Jo Gohlke from the Cesar Chavez Library, Gabriel, the Black Lotus, who has graciously given us the idea for the title *Sun Shadow Mountain* and Lorrie Salvetti who has written the dedication for our book.

Most importantly, we would like to show our appreciation to our families, for their undying support and encouragement. I, Nikki Quismondo, would like to thank my two beautiful children, Joseph Hernandez, for his enthusiasm and support, as well as his contributions to the book and Cicily Hernandez, for her typing assistance with the table of contents. I'd also like to show my gratitude to the spirit of my late grandparents, who have given me the strength and courage to follow this through, Tillie Quismondo and Julio Quismondo. A special thanks is commended to my other two wonderful grandparents, Ray and Eleanor Montanez, my parents, Irene and Joe Quismondo, and the rest of my family, Cammille, Federico and Augustine Navarro, Leslie Quismondo, Deziree and R.J. Whitfield, Christina and Marcos Nunez and Janet Maun.

I, Donald R. Anderson, would like to thank my parents, William and Marilyn Anderson, my brothers Andrew and David Andersen (they adopted the ancestral spelling) and sister Lynette Marston and their families, for their support through the artistic endeavors and their appreciation for the publications. I'd like to show my appreciation to my friends who have also shown enthusiasm for our book, thanks for keeping the momentum going!

Finally we would like to commend the people who admire poetry, who come to read and/or listen to the poetry and open mic events, the people who publish like we do, big and small, and above all, YOU! Thank you for reading our book and spreading the word and bringing it to life!

Earth, Water, Fire, Wind,
embrace these forces
for they are not only around us,
they are within us
— Lorrie Salvetti

Table of Contents: Poetry and Prose

Page

Part One: SUN

Page

Part Two: SHADOW

Page

Part Three: MOUNTAIN

Page

Table of Contents: Artwork and Photography

SUN

Gail Lee White

Dawn

In the east the dawn waits impatiently
The sky is only slightly less dark at first
The coming day still lays below the horizon
The air wet with dew in anticipation
At first a watercolor blue
A lighter wash of cobalt in the sky
Deeper pools of shadow on the ground
Slowly green emerges from the darkened trees
It is now that the birds awake
Sleepy calls from tree to shrub
The clouds above the horizon
Blush palely from gray to violet
Then pink kisses them fully awake
The light grows slowly
As if to steal into our eyes
Without being noticed
And it works
Look away for only a moment
And the whole picture changes
The eyes as inadequate as words
To capture it

Dawn comes with the new day
Even if we cannot appreciate it fully
Just as life unfolds before us
Even if we do not comprehend its meaning

Nikki Quismondo

Blooming Mestizos

There is a Pacific Islander from an Ilicano tribe
A man, coming on the boat...it is grandpa,
Speaking Tagalog
Brown like root beer
Coming to California,
Relative of Mexico,
Where there are valleys for work...

In the springtime, flowers blossom,
Pieces of fruit to be picked,
Sweat and dried skin like plumb,
Raisin eyes,
And sun flowers near the by,
Across the ways,
A field of lavender,
And a blue dress...

Grandma!

Dancing to the sounds of the mariachi guitars,
Her spirit, wild and fancy free,
Freedom only grandpa would want...
Blue dress like water
Cooling down the heat of the field workers,
Her wisdom is as antiquated like the Mayan Pyramids.
He picks a peach for her to taste...
She smiles because he has a weird
Filipino accent,
Even more foreign than she,
She offers him a cup of water,
Refreshing his fire inside,
And they make a Mexican and Filipino tribe, Mestizos!

With islander eyes and tropical skin,
Their children eat tortillas and chicken adobo,
Speaking Spanish in a Filipino accent,
Running through the fields being bitten by
Mosquitoes,
Sneezing from the allergies to pollen,
Scratching and sniffing and laughing,
Dancing the Mexican hat dance at the Filipino bazaars,

Grandma drinks her coffee con leche
And grandpa eats his pancit,

I listen to them tell the stories...
And grandpa talks about the nights he taught the
Chickens how to fight,
While grandma talks about the times she fell in love
With him....

They worked hard to be together,
Perhaps that is why they survived so long,
Them, building their own ancient pyramid
To be displayed in their own museum of stories.

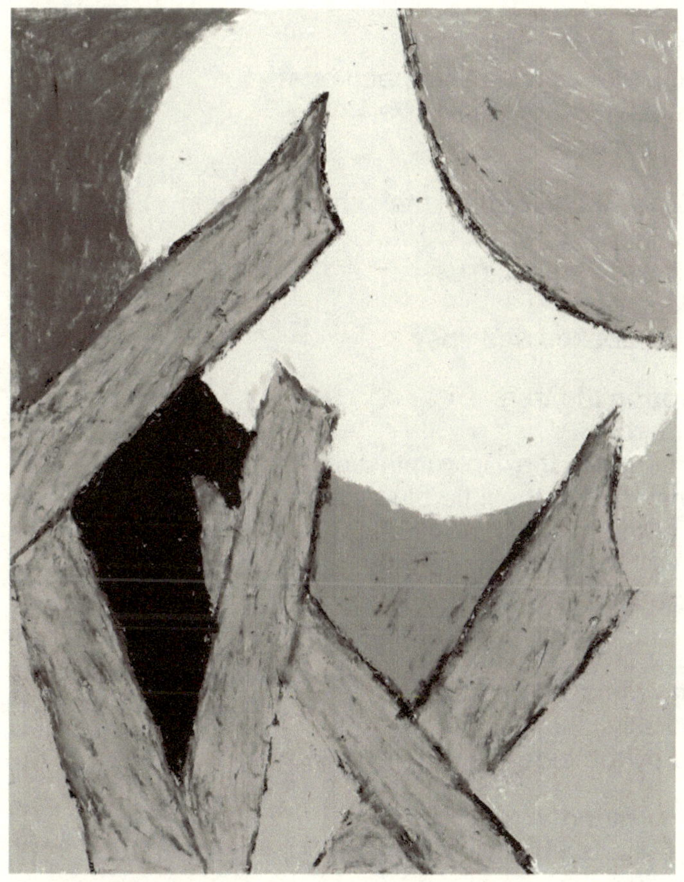

Crabgrass, by Joseph Aaron Quismondo Hernandez

Nikki Quismondo

De La Sol

Senorita margarita,
Palm tree California
Tecate y lemon
Splash of salt and sunshine
Golden spay, marinates the
Pico de gallo,

Drinking Piña Coladas,
Cozy sun spa,
Like a massage in green tea therapy,
Under the opened umbrella,
The honest valley wades in the royal blue lake,
It's cooling,
The children splash each other,
Jet skis chase the waves from the speed boats,
Carlos Santana playing *Oyo Como Va*,
Then *Black Magic Woman*,

The mothers plunk sun screen on their children's skin,
The men are fishing,
The elders wear large sunglasses
And wicker looking hats,
The young lovers, soaked and tipsy,

We hang a mirror on the tree,
Take out the paperbacks,
Put the tooth brushes in the Ziploc plastic bags,
And have organic food in the little blue ice chest, in which, we'll also
Use for a seat, a hand washing unit, and
A place to put our chess board, for later, after the
Hiking and mediation,

In the night, there are bonfires,
Children roasting marshmallows,
Story telling and silly jokes
Wisdom shared by the elder folks

And before the night trimmings,
They will all be bounded by the moon and the stars without
Thought or prejudice.

Donald R. Anderson

Shimmer

Squinting upward
to see a plane
wondering who's
looking down
wondering of
the distances crossed up above us
and of wandering places
in dusty markets
and noisy crowds
full of color
full of mischief
misplaced in time
still as sacred
looking for foreign love
looking for another life
where will I take you
to see the sights
where will you take me
beyond the sun
to a sandy beach
and wade hands held
smiling at roar of water
loving the caress of our still young bodies
in new places
I want to take you.

Marie J. Ross

The Brook

Cool stones awaken his feet,
he feels them eating moss
that feed them muddy
adventure.

Robin red breasts flutter for
his morning respite, as
moods of sunrise
breeze through.

Scent of blooming flowers
float on vernal grass,
his nostrils inhaling
the freshness.

Water ripples from strokes
of sun, his ears hearing the
motion, as he stands in
awe of its soothing
sound.

Natures melodies sing arias
to the regions of his soul, as
cerebral odyssey treads
lightly on the spirit
of himself.

Marie J. Ross

Butterflies

Butterflies flutter with wings,
of naked veins ashen on tumble
of spring air.
I watch their acrobatics,
their flash of sudden dodging
from bush to stem.
Black bellied bees pollinate,
as swift winged butterflies open
wings, closing them again on green.
They rest on watered vines, dressed
in orange and brown vests, as sun's
energy warms them to fly.
Each time my garden shovel digs,
scent of blossom unfurls, butterflies sails
to my nostrils.
And when twilight folds their wings in,
quiet night case, I hang my tired gloves
on thoughts of tomorrow's butterflies,
and garden green.

Gail Lee White

Liberty Road

The first days of summer
I head my car towards the east
The east where the orchards lay
The vineyards in their tended rows
Soon the hills begin
I can already sense the river
Though I cant see it yet
Cloaked by the ancient oaks
Surrounded by river willow and cottonwood
As I follow the road
To my special place
The place where I can find the egrets
And hear the bullfrogs love song
The shinning river on one side
The fecund swamp on the other
All manner of life thrives here
The turkey hen with her clutch of chicks
Crosses the road slowly
Unafraid of cars and fishermen
She seems to feel herself a queen
As if this place is hers alone
The river is strong here and cold
With the taste of snow still in its currents
I worry for a while about the teens
Taking a swig from a bagged bottle
Then vaulting into the icy water
So beautiful and so treacherous
Even more beautiful than their healthy young bodies
And stronger than they will ever be
Beautiful but merciless to the those foolish enough
To take her for granted
I offer a soft word of warning
Knowing they will not listen
They are invulnerable with the surety of youth
All I can do is pray that today is not the day
The day they discover how vulnerable we all are
To the whims of fate

Back on the road again
Don't tell me how environmentally unsound this is
My hiking days are long past
And I will not end my days in front of the television
I move from place to place
River road, Jack Tone, lone highway
And my favorite Liberty road
Chasing summer, hunting the last flowers of spring
Finding scattered pieces of my youth
Spent on the roads and rivers of California
When I am gone scatter my ashes on the Tuolumne river
But save a few for liberty road.

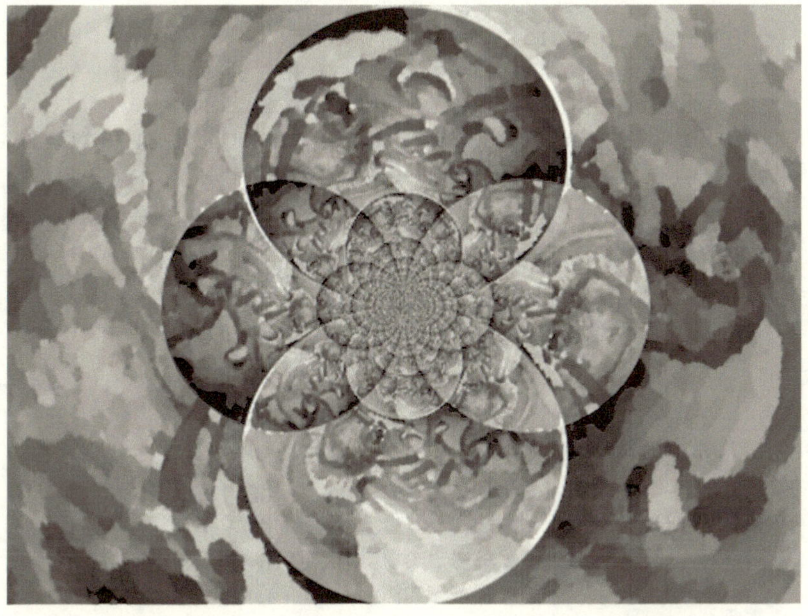

Vineyards Polarized, by Donald R. Anderson

Wayne Robinson

But She Still Loves Me

The wind of time has blown through her hair
Dyes and rinse hide the graying there
Guys no longer stop to wink and stare
But she still loves me,
Yes, she still loves me.

Her step is neither as quick nor as light
She can't wear her old jeans, they're too tight
And if I tell her that, it'll start a fight,
But she still loves me,
Yes, she still loves me.

We don't dance much anymore like we used to
The music we like to hear is no longer new
We don't attend concerts because our dollars are few
But she still loves me,
Yes, she still loves me.

She can still find things to laugh about
In me especially, that's no doubt
I think she's still trying to figure me out
But she still love me,
Yes, she still loves me.

We count calories and carbs to watch our weight
It's very seldom we manage to stay up late
But when it's bedtime, I can hardly wait!
Cause she's still loving me,
Yes she still loves me.

Marie Riepenhoff-Talty

Sunbather's Villanelle

As sun seeps in and out my skin—
in golden sensuality;
my greed for it becomes a sin.

Its warmth invades; bronze dreams begin
to ferry me to solar space;
as sun seeps in and out my skin.

When thick, black clouds force gray shade in,
I shiver with my addict's need.
My greed for sun; a mortal sin.

Supine or prone; like yang and yin—
it's all the same, I lust for it.
as sun seeps in and out my skin.

My body's shape, both fat and thin—
an Aztec soul, a burning husk.
My greed for it remains a sin.

Oh grant that I like Seraphim
will be on high at heaven's beach.
My wings transparent let sun in—
where greed's a nonexistent sin.

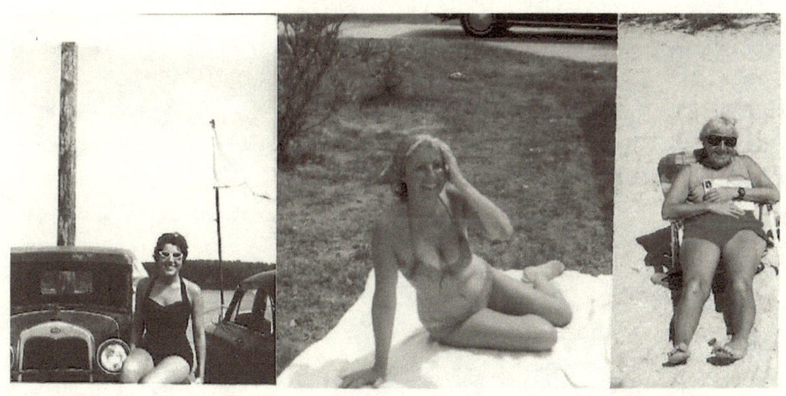

Courtesy of Marie Riepenhoff-Talty

Jeanine Stevens

DAYDREAM AT DAYBREAK

Too cold for instant plunge
this autumn morning.
Cautious as a cat, I creep
in checking the depth.

The pool, always in shade
this early, blends teal
and aqua into turquoise.
Olive spotted oak leaves tiptoe
across the still surface.

All this color is like
a monotone seascape, except
for the scent of hibiscus, fleshy
papaya, and thick coconut milk
the Samoan's say hold a man's seed.

Waves surround my feet
in a green wind, air and water
indistinguishable one from the other—
a soft caress. I think I see

a lost continent, shafts thrusting
upward, but look again—just emerald
clouds in front of a sleeping sky.

I grab my mattress, slice through
glass, try the backstroke,
Ricardo Montalban in tow.

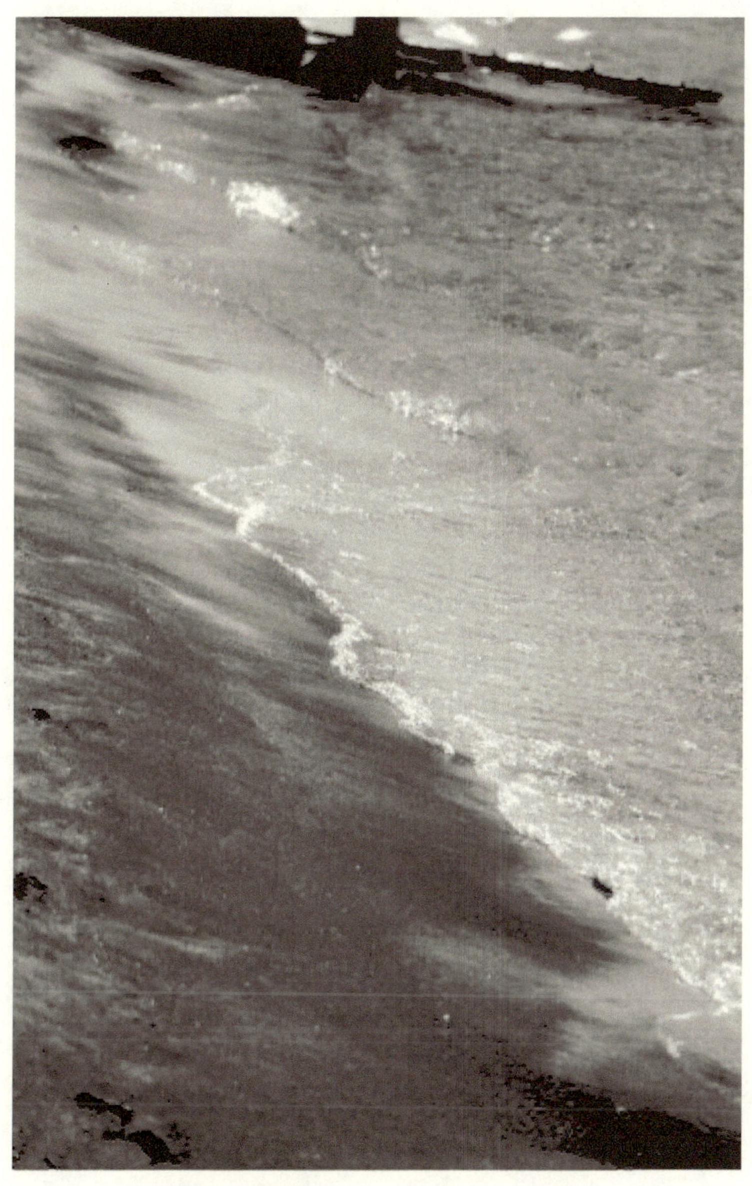

Tahoe Shore, by Reina Hutchison

Lance Wesley Hudson

My Green 1970 Pontiac Firebird

With the slight twist of the wrist it ignited
Into a muffled distinct steady rumble
The very sound that gave it its identity
Many were made but few had.....it
This car knew I respected it
I wouldn't push it any further then
It would ever push me
The responsibility of horsepower was sobering
Even when I had a few I knew
However I must admit on one occasion
I stumbled upon foolish courage
The kind of courage that breeds regret
I wanted to see which of us would back down first
on that night I pushed it
As my heart bounced around in my chest
I realized it had more then I could ever use
I was willing to come along for the ride
No matter how strong my pride
I loved my green 1970 Pontiac Firebird
Enough to never push it like that again
Although I don't drive it anymore
I miss that distinct rumble
That was just a twist of the wrist away.

Patricia Wellingham-Jones

Apple Blossoms at Eye Level

The dirt road curls up like a twisted
ribbon dropped on a mountainside. A farm in tatters
survives beside a stream. Apple blossoms at eye level,
orchard below, pink buds rich with promise
spread in misty warmth.
The orchard once produced tons of dark
winy Hungarian fruit, so deep when polished
the apples were almost black. Stunted as the old trees,
today's residents hunch thin shoulders
in faded shirts over root-matted soil. The children
scramble through branches like squirrels,
play dolls under the drooping boughs of a neighbor's tree.
They chop firewood, muck out the stalls,
pelt each other with unripe apples.
Ride the school bus smelling of horse, and share
cigarettes and marijuana behind falling-down barns.
Are they the last generation to live on the land?
Perhaps
some hazy spring morning we should stop and gaze
on apple blossoms at eye level
before they are gone.

Taylor Graham

GOLD RUSHES

We camped here stream-side
where the waters roil and riffle
red-scaled with salmon
leaping from the lock of tides,
up rock-falls, homing
in golden summer
to die.

Elizabeth Parrish

Catfish Grille
published in Lavender Fields

My car lost a few hubcaps
The other day,
It was a '49 Lincoln Coupe
Two Door Classic
With thick silver streaks
And large chrome fenders
With a catfish grille,
Painted a deep dark blue.
For years it had rolled out of my garage,
And waited patiently for its polish.
Grandpa would come over to help,
And he always carried plenty of rags.
He'd start on the front chrome,
I'd do the back;
It was our most rewarding project.
Then it would start to purr
As we headed up North
Getting frisky as it
Passed Rockport and inhaled
The salt air,
Watched sunbathers on the beach
And flirt with Cadillac's on the corner,
As we pulled in for a lighthouse view.
It was a mutual endeavor
That wings took flight that night,
As it watched the evening sky
Put on a velvet dress.
Then suddenly another coupe
Came coasting down the hill
And parked in front,
Which gave it quite a thrill.
Then they began to converse
And decided they would cruise,
Along boulevards,
Passed city lights,
Passed stars shining bright,
And checked into a quaint hotel
Where they cuddled for the night.

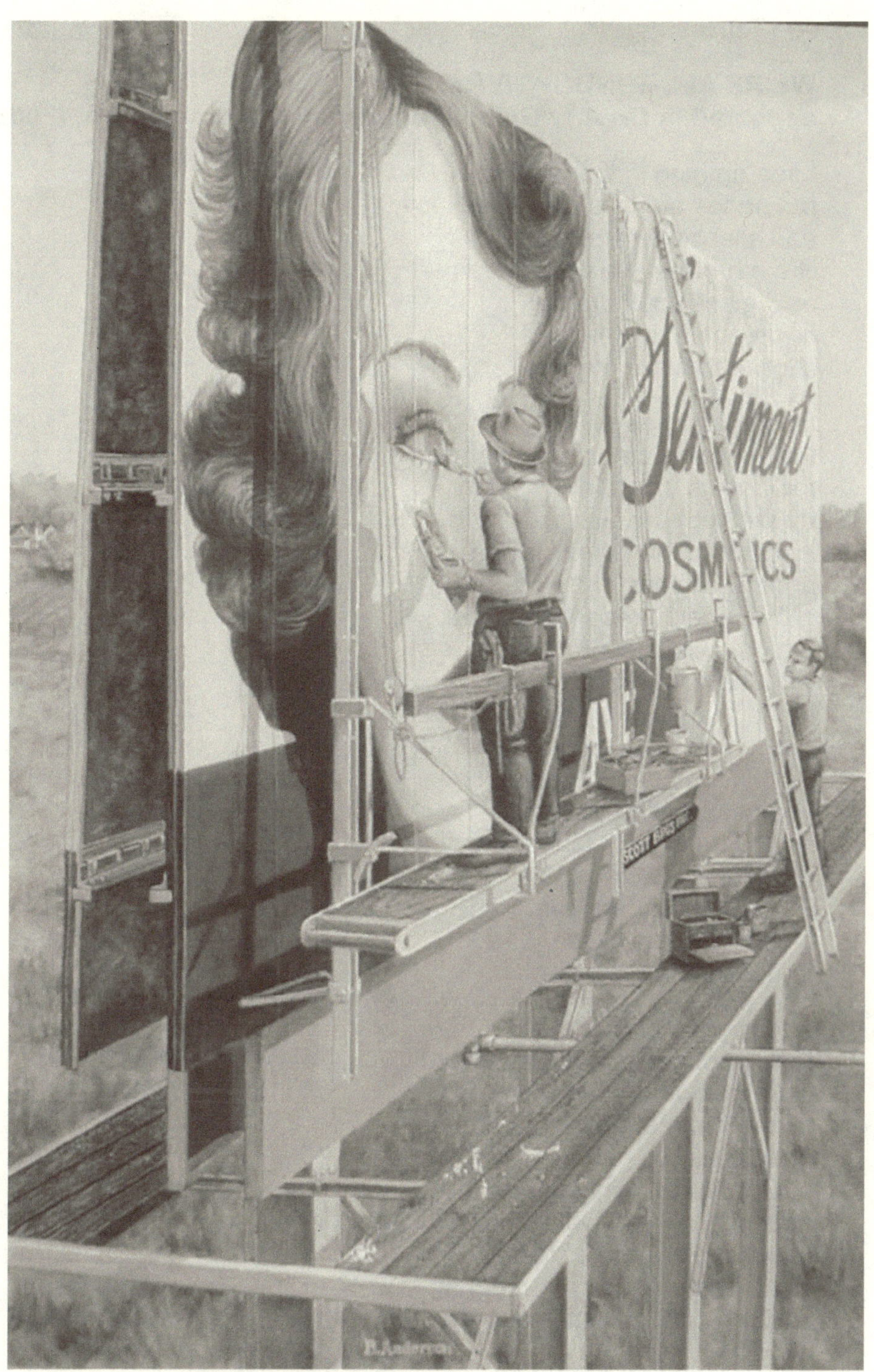

Bigger Than Life, by William Anderson

Joe Tetro

WE'RE ALL SUNDOWNERS
appeared in *On Any Given Wednesday,* Bakersfield CA, (2006)

I see nothing in the window
but panes of glass illegible as ice,
and silence enters me
like a brother I've never seen—
as if glass could freeze,
or preserve, a view and
allow it to enter me forever…

Rose branches scratch
the window screen. A flicker pecks
for insects on the ash tree
by the septic tank.
And out of the deep silence,
another silence
grows even deeper within me,
until it soundlessly merges
with the evening
in the branches of the trees, and,
way off in the west, a fast setting
sun flattens out like a gumdrop
against the hilltops,
its pink burgundy blood bleeding
into the white clouds
the way wounded love
bleeds into the lives
that lovers leave behind.

The ragged hills of clay,
their fractured water-forged skulls
worn smooth
as the teeth of gaunt old horses,
push their lips
up around the sinking sun,
and, sitting in the window,
I hear the silence echoing
within me, my internal organs
existing only by faith—

And listening to branches
stirring in a restless breeze,
and feeling darkness

touching, and brushing softly
against me, I realize
how every waking moment of life
is caught between the unheard beating
of some creature's heart,
and the silence
of it's body heat
returning to the darkness
in the dust.

Tomorrow I'll arise
with the world still wrapped in darkness,
and with my twenty gage
I'll walk across a field of dry corn stalks,
toward the gulch—
carved by waters
fleeing the hills
before civilizations arose;
and waiting for predawn
feeding flights of geese, I'll hide
behind a pile of weeds,

I'll hear my grandma telling
about times of drought
when grasshoppers came in clouds
and blotted out the sun, and chickens
went to roost at noon.
And, just minutes later,
how the sun came out again,
and the branches of lofty old trees
had been stripped clean
of all their leaves.

Every moment of the dance in the dust—
between light and darkness,
hunger and harvest,
eating and being eaten—
is precious if you think about it;
the awesome turning of energy
into heat, and heat back to dust—
the dilemma seen in the eyes—
the silence within…never more
than a breath away.

Another dance in the dust,
the hunt—not for meat,
but for the death of a brother
I've never seen, *his* return to silence,
his bleeding back into the milk-
white wrappings of the tissue paper clouds—
wistful nomads in the vast blue sea of sky,
again the bleeding: the inner terrain
of myself I've never seen—a perspective
as old as the fractured skulls of the hills
over whose evening horizon
each of us—in his, or her, turn—
will someday follow the sun.

Donald R. Anderson

Take me with you

I want to follow you to your destiny
and see it all fall together like some cosmic event.
To taste meals with you,
to listen to beauty with you,
to see the clouds churn together like furrowed brows,
touched by the majestic fate-maker's purpose.
To be there with you.
To live through it next to you.

The Libra and The Pisces

He dreams of her in oil paint
She dances on his heart with sneakers
He wishes for her fishy fins
She pleases him with seductive words and motion
He loves her more than the ocean
She cares about Henry Miller and music
He needs her like water, like air.

Donald R. Anderson

Nikki's Comet

I see you now and then
in a blaze of brilliant snow,
but when the sun circles round again,
you are faded by the majesty of humility.
Touched by fire,
you fling yourself into the sky.
And as I watch you,
I long to feel the reason you know why.

Starlight

When we are born,
we see things for the first time
and get a glimpse of something beyond ourselves.

What will I do in my life?
I want to give it my best shot
at making a difference
and try to change the world.

Each of us is born under a canopy of stars,
each and every one has the same chance of changing things.

One person,
can change one person,
that will change one person, then...
movement.

Nikki Quismondo

Opus

Needlessly, thumbing through the libretto,
I sink between the lines, soaking the air,
I want to breathe out illusions,
Make the paper wet with emotion,
Bring the orgasm to its feet!

I want to write a solid heart muscle,
Hold the manuscript, sense its weighty root,
Become impregnated with terms,
Stand upon the meaning of life's Crux,
Give birth to a major Opus.

Expose every incandescent request,
Share a mango like a writing fetish,
Tasting vowels, licking the paper...
Compose the juggler of expressions,
Split my hyper-sensitive days!

I want to stretch the whitish article,
Breed a phase of the gist, allegorical
Grow intimate with the reader,
Articulate the achy pleasure.
Hem the pages into my skin.

Donald R. Anderson

Godzilla VII

I wonder if Shakespeare drank coffee
and brewed upon it in fiery contemplation.

Stephen M. Wilson

The 3 suns align
Behind the man-made moon
Alpha's first eclipse

Lorrie Salvetti

Voices of Children

The wisdom found
through the voices of children
should never be taken lightly.
For it is within
these innocent voices
the most profound of truths
can be heard.

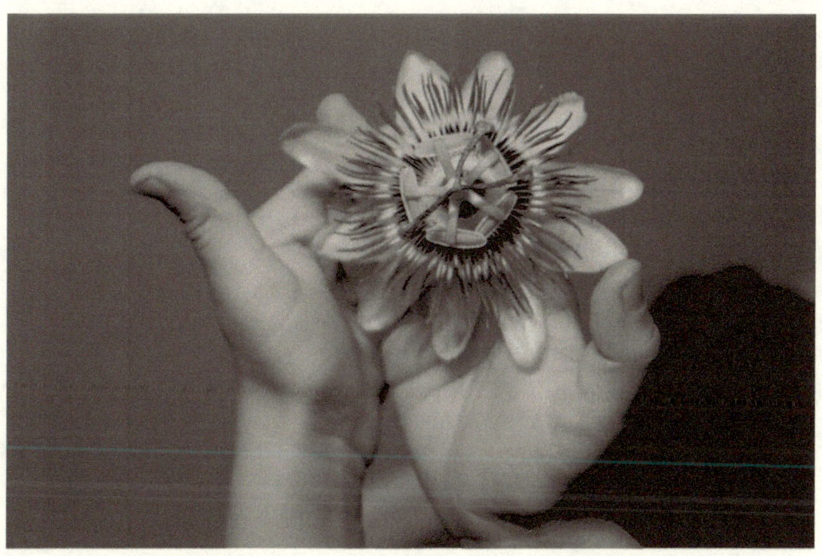

Petals of Life, by Reina Hutchison

Nikki Quismondo

Autumnal Equinox

In the celebration of the Autumnal Equinox,
The children suck the honeysuckle juice,
The sunlight feels like lemon balm,
The elders drink dandelion coffee,
There is a basket full of blue sage,
Sweet Cicely rising in the weeds,
A sugary aroma from the pumpkin cakes;
Pleasurable as the lovers watching the tangerine sunset.

There's a festival at the farmer's market,
Wine tasting,
Smoked Gouda cheese for sale,
Organic foods,
Lavender lotions,
Silk scarves and wind chimes.

In the warm dim-lighted house,
Grandma cooks with the orange and yellow squash,
Father's hammering away in the garage,
Mother's placing daisies on the table,
The girls are dressed in ruffles and satin bows,
The boys, slacks and woolblended sweaters,
My sisters bring their favorite dishes,
Everyone take place in the preparation…

There is a singular truth about the harvest time…

Family.

Mable "Jimi" Choice

Soul Food "Munchin"

Ok, I Confess...

I had me some...
Greens and Blackeyed Peas,
Hot water cornbread,
Macaroni and cheese,
Mysteriously hot seasoned rice
with mushrooms,
Superb seafood gumbo,
BBQ chicken, fried chicken, lemon
cake, peach cobbler...
Need I say more?
"Somebody put they foot in it!"
Oops! I almost forgot the red Kool-aid...

PLEASE teach the children to cook
Let's NEVER let go of this wonderful
legend of SOUL FOOD
The kind that puts meat on the bones
Thank you SOUL sisters and brothers
for the love

I admit,
I ate for fo' days without cooking'!
And it was soooooo goooood
Left-overs are the BOMB!!!!

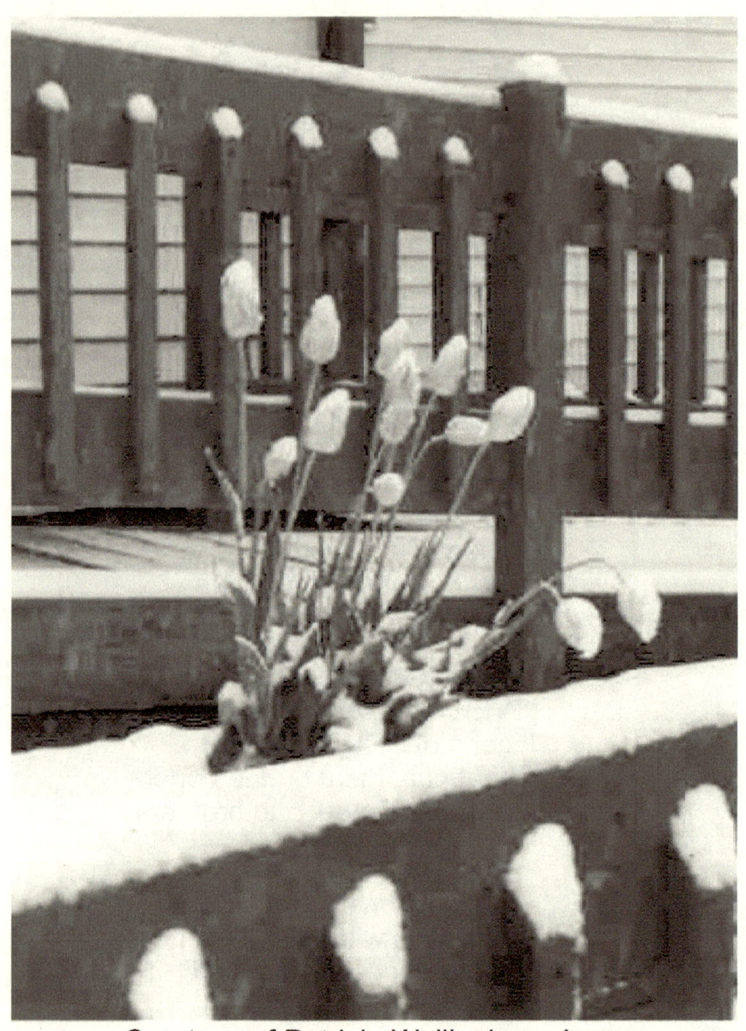

Courtesy of Patricia Wellingham-Jones

Donald R. Anderson

Captured soul in a photo you hold

The flicker of spirit in between
the sunlight warm and the shadow cool
is a missing self external
a second life
an absorbed essence entered
a transformation
without remembering before the birth
this life
is a snapshot.

Jean Claude Crhi

Untitled

When a heart is beautiful like a flower, it opens up in the morning!

Untitled

There is the road that leads to the glory of love! I will take a step to the summit of the mountain, and the joy of the sun that was hiding its grace will kiss my face... my heart will be filled with the knowledge of your Love!

Marie J. Ross

Thank You For Touching My Soul

A cold night, his eyes strained to stay open,
gray sky drew curtains across his vision,
he shuts them on the whir of night.

Captured in the blur of dream, her lips press
a kiss on his earlobe, and though she lives
in bounds of heaven, his lips found
a pathway to hers.

No longer did he feel trapped behind numb silence,
or the subconscious doorknob unturned,
her surreal touch unlocks all those cold nights.

She enters his recollection of times, when tide rolled
softly to shore, sand a cool tease on their sandals
as seagulls flapped wings to ocean operas

And from the warm and wanting land of the boudoir,
her radiant face lit candle glow, flickering
like amber pulses over their size.

Much too soon, fingertips raised his lids to reality,
and from Eden's space of Seraphim,
she whispers,
"Thank you for touching my soul."

Marie J. Ross

The Day of My Heart

June 1st
the day of my heart,
when we kissed like cling peaches,
on a summer's rendezvous of trees.
Emotion played songs as we gazed
deep into our eyes.
My long white glove spoke to you
saying,
"Slip gold band on her finger, so there
will be one."
You looked at the gold with meaning
and pride, smoothing it and rubbing
my love into its luster.
We saw only each other.
The preacher's words sailed through,
like a breeze on our forever sea of love.
Oh our wedding day, oh our wedding
night, heat revolved in the arms of purple
passion that night,
as sigh of love's completion stole our souls.
June 1st...
The Song of Our Life!
The Day of My Heart!

Marie Riepenhoff-Talty

Leaving To Find The Sun

Place the flat end into the buckle;
pull the strap tight.

Through the small rectangular window,
its rounded edges soften the view;

seemingly uninhabited, tiny
Levittown matchbox houses—

hundreds in dust-colored
checkerboard squares;

a garter snake river running below
white icing-topped toy mountains,

that move in and out of
shadow—like my life;

banking and climbing—
looking for the sun.

Donald R. Anderson

Wrinkles in the space time continuum

Retracing my steps
like I have,
I feel normal...
But once in a while,
in a strange new place,
I feel I have been there.

Perhaps I have lived
some ancestral memory over.
Perhaps I have an imagination gone too far.
Perhaps I want to connect to something so bad,
that something clicks like a gear into place.
And I am enchanted into déjà vu.

Lance Wesley Hudson

Twisted Walnut Tree

Suspended precariously
On the twisted branches of youth
I see what could be
In the glowing orb of light
Dancing on the placid horizon
Care free
Content to be lost
In the reverie of truth
Is that simple
Just to be
Without doubt or fear
As the years unfold
Untold stories
Write themselves
As I delve into
Yet another dream
Suspended precariously
On the twisted branches
Of that old walnut tree

Donald R. Anderson

Ode to a squirrel

Squirrel, whom looks at me with intent eyes of discovery.
You are among the surviving guardian angels
of mankind's war on the ecosystem,
unintentional result of consumption values.
I pray for your continued existence,
for upon it our balance depends.

Donald R. Anderson

Longing for summers past

Catching wind in my hair
holding the tree limb like a friend
that I couldn't let go
resting in the peaceful quiet orchard
light flickering through the leaves
dazzling the ground.

I hear dogs bark
and the chirp of baby birds in the next tree
wind in my ear
soft and caressing
the wind follows me everywhere
it knows my longing for
the in between space
of summer
where only time is with me
and places are far
except for the experience
of sunlight laughing.

Where do the birds
fly to when they are out of sight?

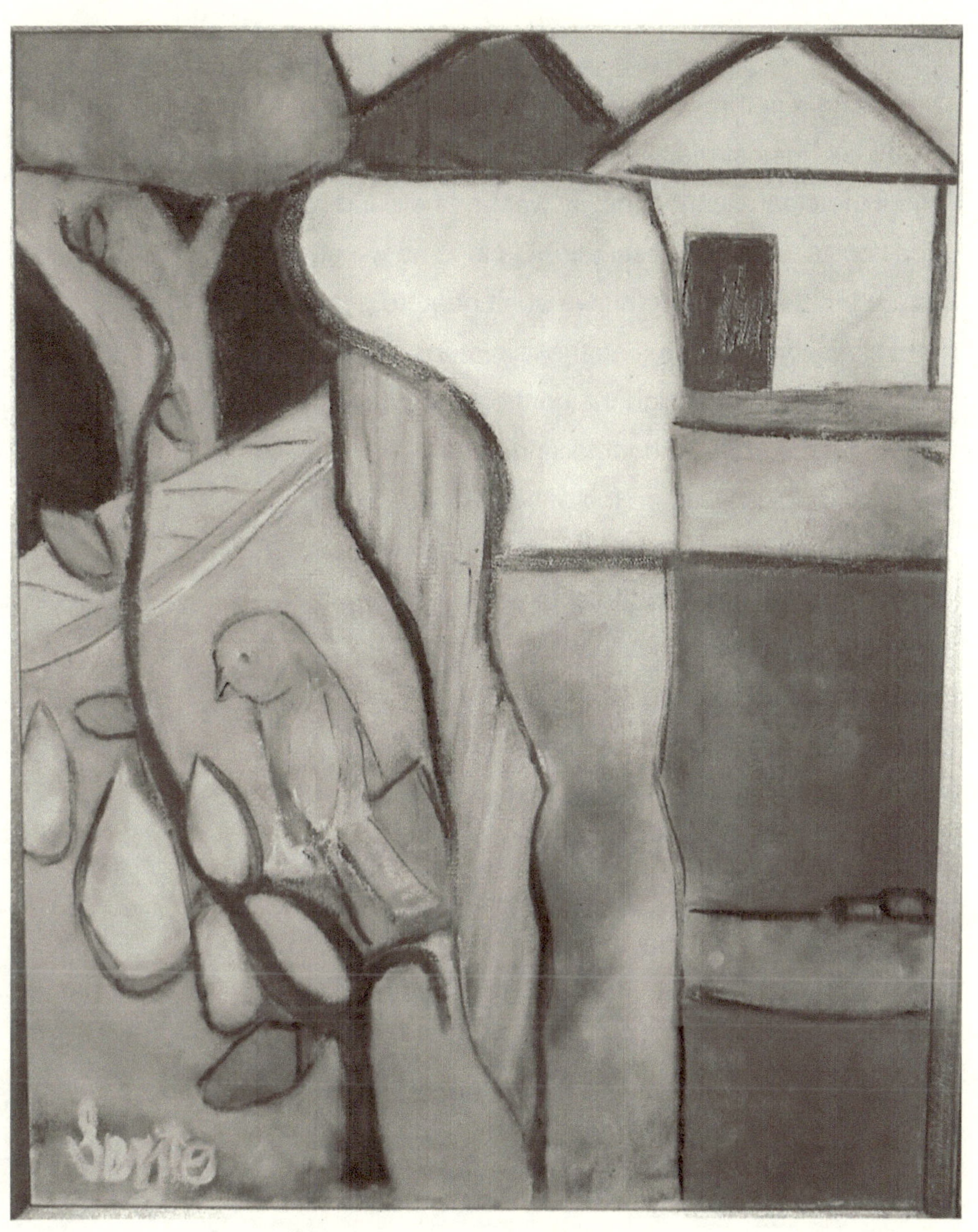

Rain on Bird, by Sergio Navarro

Wayne Robinson

Traveling

The setting sun throws a rainbow on the bellies of overhead rain clouds.
She slides against me like rain drops running down the window
I smell the clean scent of newly washed hair and hide my desire.
I don't care about our destination as long as we get to go.
It is the trip that's important, we don't need to get there.
Night closes in around us as the rain starts to fall.
Moonlight distorts through the spattered windows
Enjoying each other without talking at all
She's lying against me on top of her pillows.
I roll down the window and turn off the radio
To smell the fresh rain in the cool air
and listen to the ocean while we go
Feeling the wind blowing our hair.
She snuggles tighter, her head against me
Pulls my jacket over her goose-bumped knees
Darkness covers over the scenery
But the headlights dance in the trees.
I love a trip with a special someone
A special reason to remember the distance
Happy fun times and a surprise outcome
With carefree smiles always in abundance.

Wayne Robinson

No Tools Here

Letting the mountain stream water wash over me
Freezing cold from melting snow, still icy.
The goose bumps prickle my pink skin
Shivering, smiling, I'm skinny-dippin'

In the middle of nowhere, pine scent in the mountain air.
Took my time and walked all day to get here.
Alone, except for the chipmunks and chickadees
And the deer slinking through the brush and trees.

A sleeping bag inside a tossed up dome tent.
No care-taking, no pace-setting, no rent,
For a short while anyway, we are just a pair.
For a short time, we can savor the mountain air.

The Sierra in the early spring, snow still packed in the shadows.
Using pine boughs and denim for our sleeping pillows
And bathing in breath-removing cold ice melt
A few days exile away from the weighty tool belt.

Marie J. Ross

Fantasy's Woman

I'm woman of fantasy
Born of carnal seed.
I await in Eve's garden,
For an Adonis,
Clothed in toga
Clung to sensuality.
I fantasize on sigh,
As he moves toward me,
In motion like snail
To kiss me,
And
In breath of moon spaces,
I'm lifted to euphoria,
But
I'm only the fruit of dreams,
On a tree of unrealities,
Harvested from the seed
Of Eve's apple,
Already bitten.

Wayne Robinson

I remember love so real and pliable that I could pick it up, and it would flow through my fingers like dry sand. The love would pile up at my feet and surround me with a feeling of warmness, like the setting sun shining down in my face while I sat on the beach. I remember that warm feeling.

Every time I get the chance to close my eyes to relax, I see the smiling face of a dream that I once loved more than my own life. She radiated love to me like a hungry craving. You know the craving; the one you have when you need something sweet, but can't quite figure out what it is that you really want. I knew I needed her, she knew I needed her, and I wonder what I did wrong, what I didn't do, what I should have done, that would have made her stay. She was all I wanted, all I knew that I wanted.

The moon was as full and shining as a new china plate reflecting the sun. Silver light shone through the window, making her soft skin, look even softer, her bright smile, shine even brighter, and the love I saw, look even stronger. Was I moonstruck from the full moon, or was it the love I felt?

The summer breeze coming softly through the window screen, cooling our nude-sweaty bodies. Her head lying in the crook of my arm while she laughs and talks about the happenings of her day. I absorb her touch, melting in it, trying desperately to stay awake and hear all that she has to say.

So many places to go, so many places I wanted us to enjoy together. The old shops down Cannery Row, the sequoias of Big Trees and Yosemite, the giant redwoods of the coastal northwest, holding hands walking the paths and sidewalks of Lover's Point. Just you and I, like no one else existed. These things I dream of, I long for, I need, the togetherness, the oneness, where is the oneness?

Your meaningless words lie around my feet like a child's toys scattered on the floor during a rainy afternoon. I feel the loneliness lying on me like the weight of extra blankets on an icy-cold night.

It was so good it was frightening; each time we made love was like an adventure, a challenge to our skills and for our devotion. There was nothing else, no time, no space, no other world, nothing else except us, wrapped together like stripes on a candy cane, wonderful and sweet.

I hear the voice deep inside silently calling me home with wordless pleading. I can almost smell the kelp, the whisper of the breaking waves, and the faint sharp cries of distant gulls that keep flying around inside my mind. Home! Home! They shriek, my brain echoing their cries across my mind. The waves splash a cleansing mist that purifies my dreams and renews my spirit with fresh growth and invigorating dreams.

Nikki Quismondo

Libra Rising

I am free to the rising of Libra.
And when the waters come towards me,
I open myself to the air,
Taking in rain,
Feeling the softness,
Wanting to be soaked into clouds...

Let us always be wind and water,
Sail out into the horizon
Take pleasures upon the cherry blossom sky,
Catching wet mists and zephyr glides.

Let us taste liquid motions,
Like jazz and *Bird* and song.
With whetted appetite, and elated tongues.
Let us become the rolling naked rain,
With grand and distinct plummets,
Like a waterfall symphony,
Like sun showers in the Saint Helena vineyards.

From the daydreaming, I breathe daisies,
Dance in the wet plumes,
Take night swims in the Nile,
Rub my body in peppermint oils,
And wait for your Grand Trine.

Shonda Renée

On Friction

His energy parts
me through the middle and I
open up like Earth
yielding to temperatures
greater than can be contained.

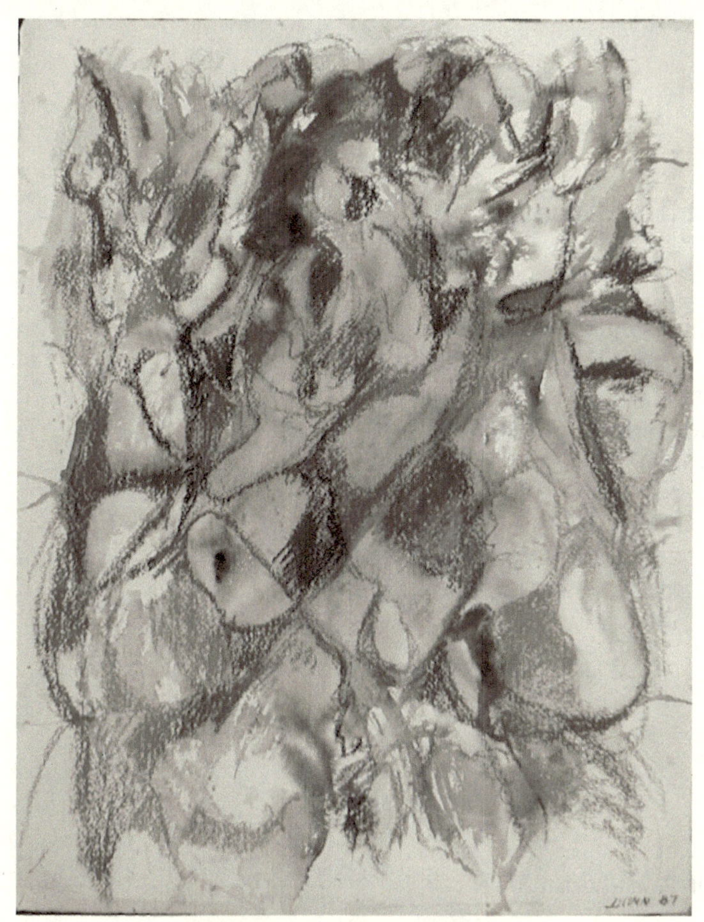

Untitled, by Tommy Dunn

Lance Wesley Hudson

Lust

The waves of lust delicately lap
At the shores of innocence
Sending a quivering shutter
Through insatiable throbbing flesh
Pounding rhythms rise
Into ominous waves
Forcing unwitting pawns
Through the ache of ecstasy
Frantically flailing into
The raging currents of passion
And empty hourglass is filled
With timeless sensations
Faint echoes of youthful bliss
Lost but unforgotten.

Patricia Mayorga

The Clearing

Billows north I drift to you
sink my soul in coolness blue
rest a weary self, my need
your bleeding heart will be my lead.

When in blindness I do slip
to shadows fogging angel's tips
horizon sends your loving smile
reminding me, you were there
all the while.

Lorrie Salvetti

Compassionate Light

Even at the darkest hour
in the midst of confusion and chaos,
there is a light that will never grow dim
this light is the miracle of human
compassion,
the presence of Angelic influence
it comes from the depths of our souls
and from the place some refer to as
heaven...
there is only the need to accept and
believe in this light
in order to call upon it and be assured of
its eternal embrace.

Marie J. Ross

Rising Sun

A bleached sky opens quietly,
lifting up a lazy disc, morning
cools sneaking over the
canopy's eye.

Yellow creams blend off serene
clouds, sliding down the blush
of sun beams, and desiring
earth's green grass.

Her yellow face is a promise,
of fruit and honey, of seed
and yields, before shades
of pewter fall.

Eyes stray from her fingers,
that dipped ginger on skin,
and watch her throat open
and consume all light
from day.

Sun rises early from bleached
sky, as we see the ticking clock
undress her, with hands
sweeping like golden
brooms.

Donald R. Anderson

40 Years

40 years
40 years—a drop in the ocean.
A little bigger but still quite the same.
A wisp of flight on blurred-edged scabbards
that are embedded in sand
on the island of our senses,
reaching out to other shores
with our hopes on understanding.
The self that one wants to know
where one creates oneself
as it creates trains of streaming consciousness.

Looking at the horizon for the first time.

Children of a cloudy blue Earth sky
fantasizing sleepy eyed on the fixed mountains
in the distant skyline.
Wishing for a better tomorrow
where they want to be
for a thousand—
count many that you can remember more—
days alive in this life, from innocent
and learning brilliance to
colder nights on the heart.
Still feeling as vibrant,
alive,
sensual,
emotional,
painful.
It is what it is to be alive.

Marie J. Ross

Deep Down Music

I listen to music
New York, Los Angeles,
Jump man hop.
Saxophone rituals
mellow, bittersweet,
wanting.
Drums are liquors
of my passion,
my feet drinking
every rhythmic beat.
And
Ivory keys
play those soulful renditions,
a carpet of notes leading
to Sangri-La.
All notes vibrate,
march off manuscripts
through
my red rooms,
through blue pulses,
and
sun pausing on my window pane.
Deep down
music is my existence
my,
New York, Los Angeles,
Jump man hop,
Where I sit in their parlors and live.

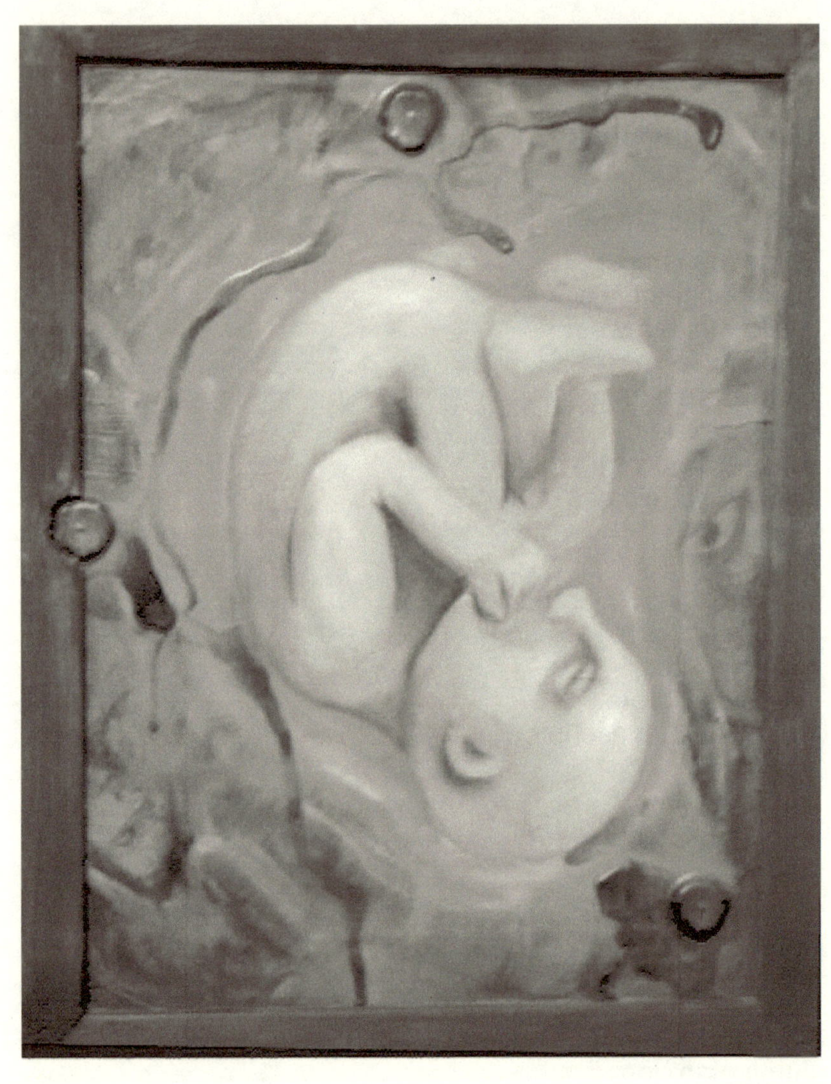

Untitled, by Charley Stockdale

Reina Hutchison

Moments of Motherhood

Her tiny hand upon my breast
Her head nestled on my shoulder.

A sigh of peace
A giggle of satisfaction
A smile of happiness.

She wraps her hand around my finger
Stands tall on my flattened palm
Unyielding trust, unending faith
In my love for her.

Eyes shine full of curiosity
Eager to learn
Knowing my face
My daughter
My light
My future
My world

Wayne Robinson

THE SPEED OF THOUGHT

The speed of thought, galaxy beyond galaxy
Beyond what the strongest telescope can see,
Walking colorful beaches hand in hand
On a nameless planet in a faraway land.

We have made love in places others only have in dreams.
Under giant mushrooms beside turquoise streams,
Inside a giant bird nest lined with quills and down,
In a bathtub warm sea surrounded by salty foam.

Nude bodies wrapped together under twin full moons
Listening to the mournful cry of the floating loons.
Watching strange night birds dance in star dust air
Like the darting bats chasing the insects there.

I miss you, new solar systems shall come and go,
Suns will set, rain will fall, and winds will blow
But you are a living dream of flesh and bone.
Good together, everyplace we go feels like home.

Now you are the dream, a memory, a love so very gone,
Though I see you daily, only a dream, passing like a sun.
My mind sees you, my arms reach, but I only touch air,
The lifetime that stands between here, and between there.

The speed of thought, you are here, then you are not,
You chase your dreams the other man you've got,
I live in stalemate, absorbed in my work, surviving.
I miss the excitement, the laughing, and mostly the loving.

We see through eyes that are the same, our dreams, our desires,
We have feelings of love that have grown from the same fires.
A hundred years, or a hundred seconds, it will always be the same
One foot, or light years away,
I shall always wish you wear my name.

Marie J. Ross

BREATHING COLORS

Stockton Arts Commission, Poetry Contest, 2000, Honorable Mention

To ingest color is to feel
the liquid of their
flesh.

To inhale their moods and
let them kiss you—
coolly.

To press your fingers on ice
blue waters, sipping calm
from sapphire skies.

And feel the dress of green
behavior or'e the land
of natures prides.

To see the scarlet brush of
sunset, from her house
of quiet dreams;

Feel the rust on leaves that
wander, breathing hard
on winter seams.

Touch the brown of mighty
trees, those kings and
lords of all the land,

And see the sunrise curve her
splendor, off the crimsoned
Goddess Hand.

So, ingest the spirit of these
colors, feel their liquid
flesh repeat;

Inhale their moods of quiet
moments and give your
soul that place to meet.

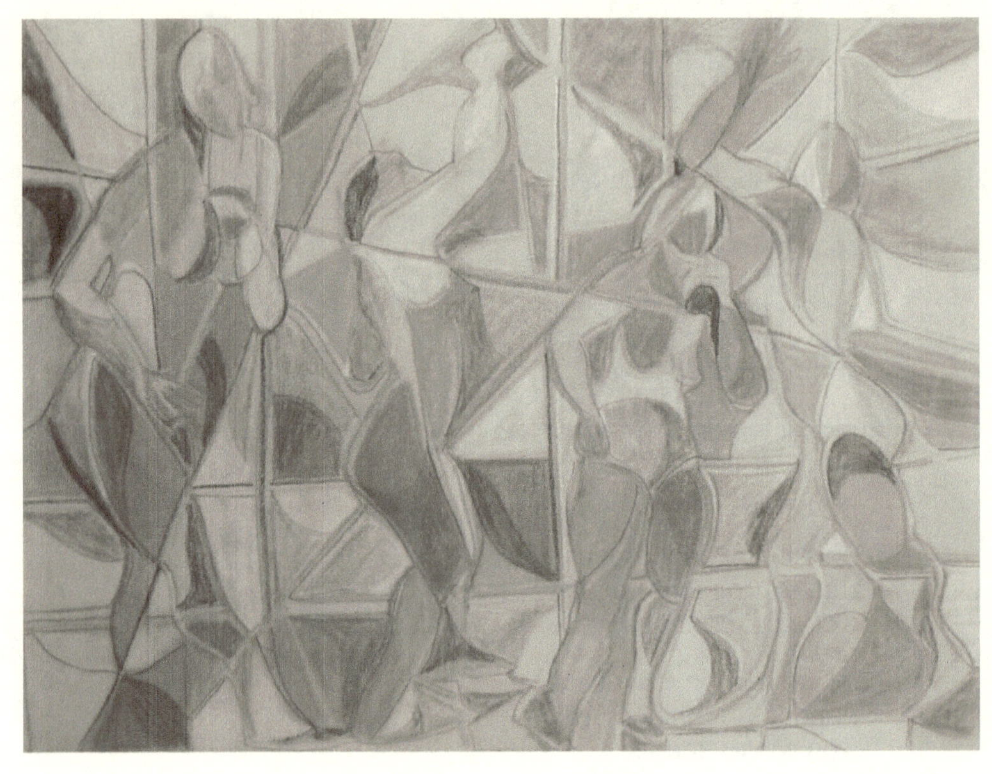

Illusions, Tommy Dunn

Taylor Graham

IRON MOUNTAIN HYPOTHESES

I was sitting by myself in the woods
writing a poem about being alone
but not lonely,
not even missing the jukebox
that makes such sweet-achy music
out of loneliness.

And now, driving home
among the solitary trees, I see
two couples beside a stopped sedan,
the driver's door wide open,
and radio country-music pouring out,

two couples in the eastbound lane
dancing a Texas two-step
in the midst of miles of forest.

Why would they choose this asphalt
for a dance-floor?

1. They're a figment of loneliness
denied/suppressed by some trite
Romanticist notion
that it's good to be alone.

2. My poem, invoking the peace
of un-jukeboxed solitude,
challenges the couple-ness
of dancers to appear.

3. In the rationalist view,
the conjunction of two-step with poem
is pure coincidence.
Anyone dancing in the middle
of the eastbound lane
should watch for oncoming traffic.

4. It's serendipity.
Take it as you will.

Wayne Robinson

Sun Shadow Mountain

Lying in the shadow of the mountain, waiting for the sun to rise
Looking out through the flap of the tent through sleepy eyes,
Listening to the singing of the tiny wrens
Thinking about getting up for my camera lens.

The stream is blanketed in floating gray mist.
I keep thinking, "It don't get any better than this."
The old joke rings in my mind like a dream.
The snow high up looks like ice cream,

Vanilla ice cream, snowy white and as cold as the morning
A flash of sunlight causes the mist to start rising
And the bouncing stream sparks and dances diamonds,
My love's eyes open and look like brown almonds.

Living in the shadow of the mountain, waiting for the sun to shine,
My love wrapped within my needful arms, suspended in time.
A moment, a millisecond, in the eternal counting of infinity,
Is ours under the shadow of the mountain on this sunny day.

Donald R. Anderson

The Land of Wanting

The green grasshoppers dance
huge legs catching the air
in the fields of wheat and grains.

I lie there
knees toward the sky
dreaming of ice cream with chocolate syrup
and streaked layers of caramel and nuts,
missing the sky-rocket-launches
pillowing upward into the bright blue
our creations destroyed hundreds of feet away
torn parachutes dangling on twigs and stray rocks.

Can you feel me here lying on rough dirt
jeans worn at the knees
neck cradled in my warm hands
as I close my eyes and escape
from that world that you knew
those dreams
painfully beautiful
of something so grand
that only we knew of them.

I long for that sky blue wisp
to ride it away.

Donald R. Anderson

Shy lizard

Critter of the dark,
shocked by sprinkler drops,
scattered into pieces
footprints across muddy lawn.

Why are you so shy,
lizard of the shadows?
Why do you fear the light,
and feel the comfort of the dark.
It answers itself in the rain,
cool upon a mid-autumn twilight.

I fancy an afterlife
among those leafs
as big as big city cars,
and wet with the velvet tears
of a mucked up biological
orgasmic sky.

Awning

As the sun rose
shade by the window,

sparkled and glimmered,
in a spectrum
then settled with green
with the full light,
book open, pages in wind,
hat on face, legs on chair, sleeping.

Lance Wesley Hudson

Vibrant Intensity

I find your vibrant intensity engaging
Turning me around like a carousel
Eternity is but a moment suspended
In mind's eye you are warm delicate waterfall
Trickling down into the deepest recesses
Of my dancing heart as we embark on our journey
Through time our designs intertwine like Ivy vines
Quietly crossing invisible lines that divide the blind
Refuse to see the vision of what could be
In this ever changing anomaly.

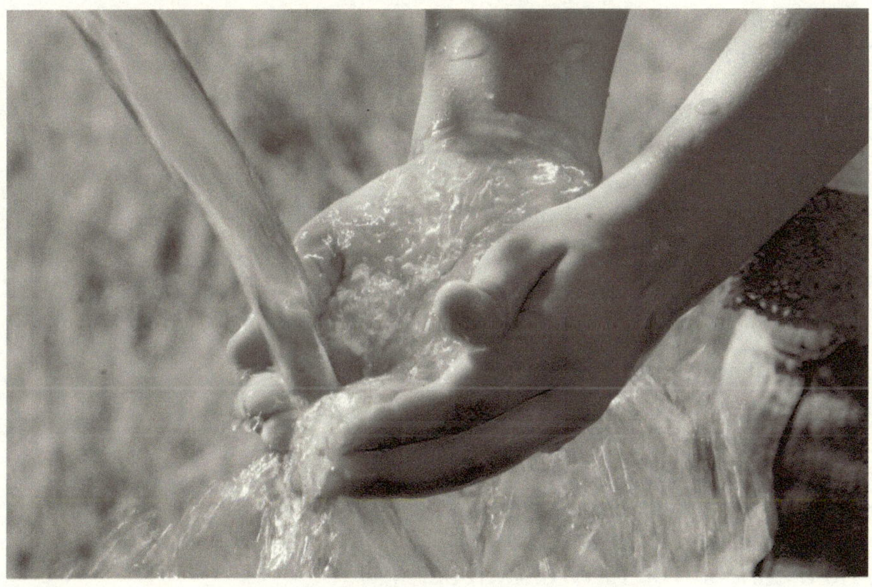

Innocence, by Reina Hutchison

Andy Pope

Sungazer

When the day dawned to your glory,
And first you faced the Sun
As it crept through the clouds
And cast their vapors in the air,
You then engaged your soldiers
On whose shoulders once She sat,
Primed to make their plunders
And their war.

Thus usurping the Sun,
We would now be fierce and free,
As the dawn broke with decision,
Though its meaning were not felt.
And how you thought yourself valiant
As you rode forth in radiance,
Never nodding to restriction
In your all-consuming fervor,
Like a page or a pawn overtaken
By the power of a promise
And yet blinded to the turns that lay ahead.

At the pinnacle of folly,
You stood boldly on the altar of blasphemy,
Your finest wish to offer.
And you flung it about like a prayer without direction,
Like a spell without the benefit of craft,
Embracing the emptiness
Your fantasies fought to fill.

Then suddenly the soldiers of the cynical
Emerged and answered wildly:
"Come joust with us!" they cried.
"There will be spectators aplenty
In the colosseum of the courageous:
Yea, even maidens whose delight
Is in the manhood you have shown us,
That thereafter we might revel
In the benefits of decadence:
Let us strip them of their chastity,
And christen them with wine!"

Then came the Queen of Space
To present you before the stars.

She is seated in the Universe,
Statuesque and stunning,
She: the subtly sounding siren
Singing canons to the lost,
Now summons you with gaiety,
Appearing as an Angel
On whose garment all the galaxies
Have tugged and felt her pull:
Yea, the greatest of the saints
Have surrendered to her gravity,
While those men who were your soldiers
Now attend to her as suitors,
And you stand, a living consequence,
Too hungry to be wise.

When She offered you an overflowing chalice
From which you were quite quick to drink,
You thus did greatly err.
For her drink became as boiling oil,
And it burned your bowels to brokenness,
That the images of her majesty
Might fade like mirages in your path.

At that She laughed,
And your former henchmen howled,
But still you gazed into the Sun,
As though fueled by your fantasy,
You thought yourself emboldened
At the moment of your misery,
Made manifest in the movements of the men
As they returned to serve Her glory,
And then stripped you of your armor,
Working wounds into your flesh,
To go untreated,
As She laughed!

And the Sun, and the Queen, and Her soldiers
All delighted in the sight
To see you drift among the doomed,
Your eyes fixed fully on the features of the faces
Of the souls whose only solace
Is to love the downfall of the unsuspecting,
And to treasure the tears of the defeated,
As among them you descended
Into the havens of the damned.

Donald R. Anderson

Passion Daybreak

On the shores of Babylon
washed in from struggles drenched
looking for love.

Arthur Miller Conference

Arthur Miller Conference
was the beginning of a new start,
only fate could have brought us together after,
in the open mic of a coffee shop.
To take the steps all again,
would I have been as bold?
I wouldn't change the past,
I'd take it just to get where we are now.
In the tears I share with you,
when you share yourself in every way,
and I open up, a flower in your angel-light.

**Watching Cleopatra While She Sleeps,
Wondering What She Dreams.**

When I walk in San Francisco,
I always look for your face in the crowd.
Something about the air's scent
makes me think of you.
When I see bricks
or when I feel hungry for sushi,
I long to share it with you.
The silver sculptures in goodwill,
glow with a precious endurance that reminds me of you.
You put this yearning in my heart,
so what do we do with it?

Donald R. Anderson

Desert Preponderances

Where can the shadows be without sunlight,
and without shadows we would be fried in sun.
The snake slithered through the sand,
aching to feel the cold of under a rock.
There is only so much of a good thing.

Tasting the salt of a beach
can be like experiencing over one's birth.
It is quite like the new sensation,
that is like you're experiencing it new,
when it first happened,
as if the gap between the re-occurrence
of said sensation
and the past,
is but a mere glass window,
carved from reality,
mistaken to be in the same reality,
as what we used to be,
who we are,
and what we always will be.

Snake slithers along the shoreline,
tasting the salt,
the clashing between dry air,
and the incoming shore.
Where one senses these things,
one transitions,
into the moment.

SHADOW

Joe Tetro

SHADOWS

dance, then creep up from behind.
You bow to the rising sun, your shadow
bows behind you. You stand up, so does
your shadow…letting you know
you're never alone. Shadows mock, guide,
and frighten, then, beckon you, and
form shady pools whose derivations
shield you from the sun.

You stop, your shadow stops, but run,
and your shadow runs with you. It
races ahead when the sun's behind you,
follows you when it's up ahead. Scraps of
darkness, shadows, but always loyal to
light. Thus the hat shades the face, and, as the
mountain switches faces at noontime, so the
shadow switch sides, forever a shifting
display of the movement of light as it tours
its great rounded highway across the sky

Oh fluid shadows, somber as the sounds of
sorrow, yet, in the most delightful way,
you tell me I'm no longer in the womb,
and not yet in the grave.

Stephani Schaefer

Letting Go

The wood table where she still sits.
Throat of the Iris. Birdsong.
The dancing shade full of bits of light.
White clouds walking.
A strong and fitful breeze.

Later, a steady wind. Leaving.
Moving uphill on a long song, breathing deep.
Dragging two hands through soil.
Tearing up grasses in the singing wind.
Swallow. Swallow grief. Swallow your heart.

The warm stone.
The massed trees slapping in the sun.
Silent acceptance.

The deep, deep sky.

Nikki Quismondo

Sailing
published in Naked Poetry

Sailing,
Watered dreams,
He,
Endless sea.
Blue reflections shape waves;
Will he stay?
Always.
When it rains,
On teardrops,
In reason imbued.
Why?
For safety,
For floating,
For sailing blue.

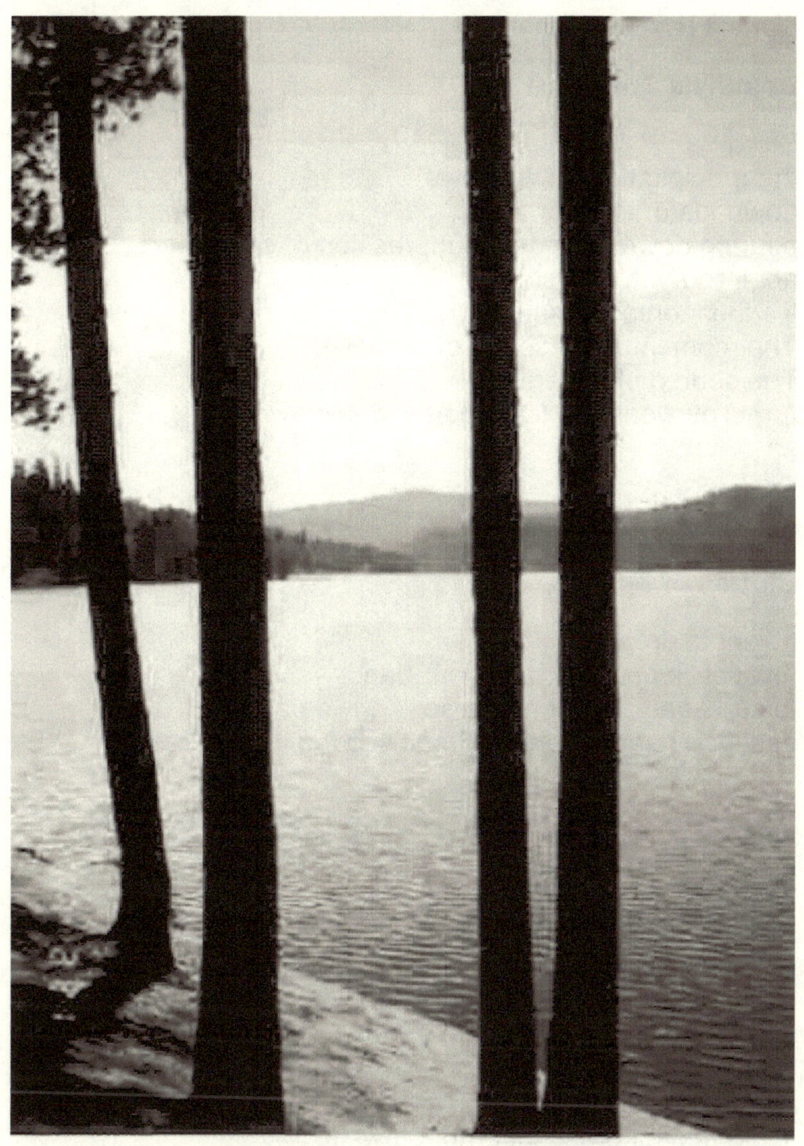

Courtesy of Patricia Wellingham-Jones

Donald R. Anderson

Destiny's Storm

Storm:
the precipitation on windows
down the drainpipe
pouring down from dark suppression of cover
not freed-yet. The storm.
It's the inertia of change.
The momentum of sense of purpose.
The source of adversity.
A mellow yearning for Utopian tomorrow.

Clouds of heaven

I want to dream in
mystical journey to hold your hand—
to curl against your hot torso like two cats
destined heartache San Francisco fog dream-scape.

Night feathers

Night feathers...
floating moon on ocean slosh of tide.

Pleasant fire in lantern
licking flames,
liquid phosphorescent amber jewels...
a pair reflecting the glow,
slipping over curves of azure phantoms
down the course of human history's tongue
to the end of the world,
looking over the stars
twisting in their glittering clouds,
falling asleep holding you close.

Patricia Wellingham-Jones

Closing the cabin for the winter

Pine shadows stripe the blacktop,
vine maples spill gold on the road,
willows dance orange tangos in the breeze
as we drive to the lake in late October.

Our voices skim across whitecaps, disappear.
Squirrels chatter, dig pine nuts out of cones.
Jays demand sandwich scraps
the year is too old to provide.

On the far shore a loon pulls down a rain cloud.
We hear the slap of rising waves on the shore.
Lightning slashes through steamy black wool,
insects shrill their alien tongues.

Around us the air explodes with sound.
The storm breaks over our heads
like soup bowls thrown at a wall and I
want to cower with the dogs under the bed.

Next morning with pipes drained, windows shuttered,
we leave in the first sprinkles of snow.
The mountain prepares itself for winter—
lake black in the coming cold, voices silent.

Joe Tetro

BEETHOVEN'S SIXTH

Dancing, whirling women, skirts a-flare,
the music cavorts, gallops, skips, stops,
and prances, the sky opens its eyes, surprised.
The river—never the same river twice—
flows to sea. The music trembles,
and shudders, temporizes, a shepherd boy's
flute echoes notes as pure as moonlight,
strings build tension, bosoms blossom
into flowers, nipples erect as stroking bows,
gray shadows edge in and fade. A
rush of upward volume then melts like
wax in a flame. Dancing resumes, and
the music swells, then fades like a setting sun,
then, like unfinished fervor, rises again,
the flute grows precocious, then fades to a
blade of grass...all stops. Eyes search
the horizon—What looms? A strange calm,
uneasy interlude, euphonious sections of
orchestra vacillate with the enigmatic
coyness of trembling anticipation...A child
swings, the music darkens as if clouds
approach, the twittering of nervous birds
is heard. Are the musicians weary? The river
moves, but doesn't move, a dubious
wistfulness comes and goes. Wine
is poured, small talk exchanged. Sleepiness
stretches out the notes the way salt water
hands pull taffy, pastel notes slide in
and out of one another. The carriage horses
grow impatient—paw the ground, and nod
anxiously, low begging whinnies
vibrating in their throats, the sky
blushes pink, a wistful flute flutters
as if calling a lover. All becomes hushed.
A sudden energy emerges on impatient
waves of rising urgency—an imperial
motif? Echoes of some epic event?
Some shaving of eternity
demanding attention?—perhaps
an army going to war...yet,
ghostlike mercurial waves
of the primordial unconscious

push up…and up…and up
against the land of consciousness—
faces in light become faces in darkness,
trouble free as a plump child,
yet stricken as madness awakening
in a mass grave. Footsteps resound
as if titans approached, earth trembles,
life is reduced to a piercing fear,
a surreal acuity—pure, purer, purest,
and, yet, even *purer*—the awesome fear
builds. Horizons erupt in fragments
that dissolve in dust. The pale sun,
choked by chaos while attempting
to sing through the clouds, is swiftly
raped by darkness. Night weeps
and rocks babies in its arms…but wait!
Perhaps…perhaps…but just perhaps,
the storms of darkness have
passed. But only perhaps. The lead violins
tease, now…other sections
still not sure, though. The wind section
wistfully hopeful. Yes!
the orchestra is fading—
the storm has passed, and we
have all been spared.

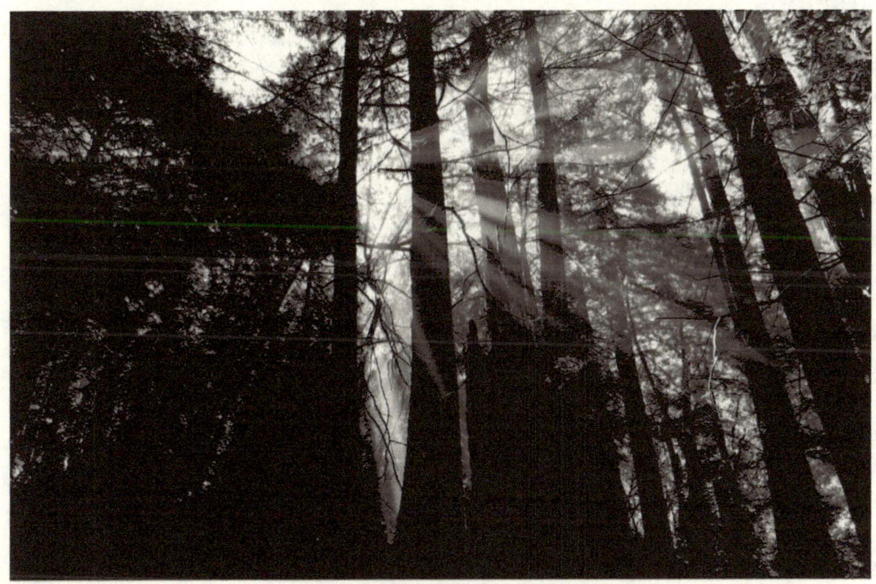

Courtesy of Reina Hutchison

Marjorie Wagler Carmack

Untitled

The wind roars a song through the old sycamore,
And the rains beat like drums on my old cabin door.
The fogs come a-driftin' and a siftin' all around,
While the water runs like rivers from the highlands on the ground.

But the fire is a-burnin' in the old barrel stove,
In the cabin all is cozy like a hand within a glove.
The Aladdin lamp is shining like the warm sun at midday,
And the babes are all a-sleepin' like the lambs upon the hay.

But there are three things a missin' in this cabin bright and warm,
When inside it is so cozy and outside there is the storm.
Three marines, the hills own children, one of them across the sea,
Oh this cabin will be heaven when they all come back to me.

Lance Wesley Hudson

Obstructions

Longing to awaken
the truth remains dormant
in the heart of a lost child
inevitable, a vital transformation
has yet to be endured
turbulent, the seas of confusion
rage into oblivious disregard
for sacred gift of life
that has been given with mercy
we break the brutal cycle of
self-indulgent disdain
obstructions to be dismissed
as twisted visions of fear
as his mercy purges
the soiled relics of truth
sacred gifts of knowledge
that ride the raging winds
into the mystery of eternity.

Patricia Mayorga

She

Soft folds crease, designing a mystery
that changes everything
        when she enters.

Small hands fit nicely into calloused ones
dying to be her
        hero.

Lace covers silk cups that he would sell his soul for;
He imagines his picture in her empty locket
        waiting.

Splendor holds a buckled shoe, that safety strap,
protecting curves that stop
        his breath.

He wills his concession, swearing his life to her
in all truth and goodness, if only given
        the chance.

Lance Wesley Hudson

Night Play

Silence the notes that
glide in on a night's whisper
slowly fade into a moon's gaze
as lost stars dance away
thoughts begin a waltz
to the wind's serenade
randomly played
constantly swayed
silent refrain
quietly fade.

Elizabeth Parrish

Soldier Listing into Port
published in Lavender Fields

There is a soldier listing into port
After a bullet struck his leg.
He floats on the rippling tide
And crawls like a languid lizard
Up into the bleached sand dunes,
Stretching his hand to light
On the straw of life,
Because that is the thought
His mind holds onto.
The ice blue eyes
Do not reflect
The coldness of his enemies.
He doesn't want
The dampness of sand
To be his tomb.
For a moment
He reflects
On the element of sand
And thinks of what might
Possibly hold it together.
His mind drifts
Among shallow pools
Of childhood
And he clings
To the life
His mother gave him.
What was it that ailing woman
Whispered?
Was it that life was too precious
To leave?
Yes, for that he would stay
And look into her hazel eyes,
Surrounded by wavy
Chestnut hair,
For she too
Was a sea of her own,
For her he would win
And come home.

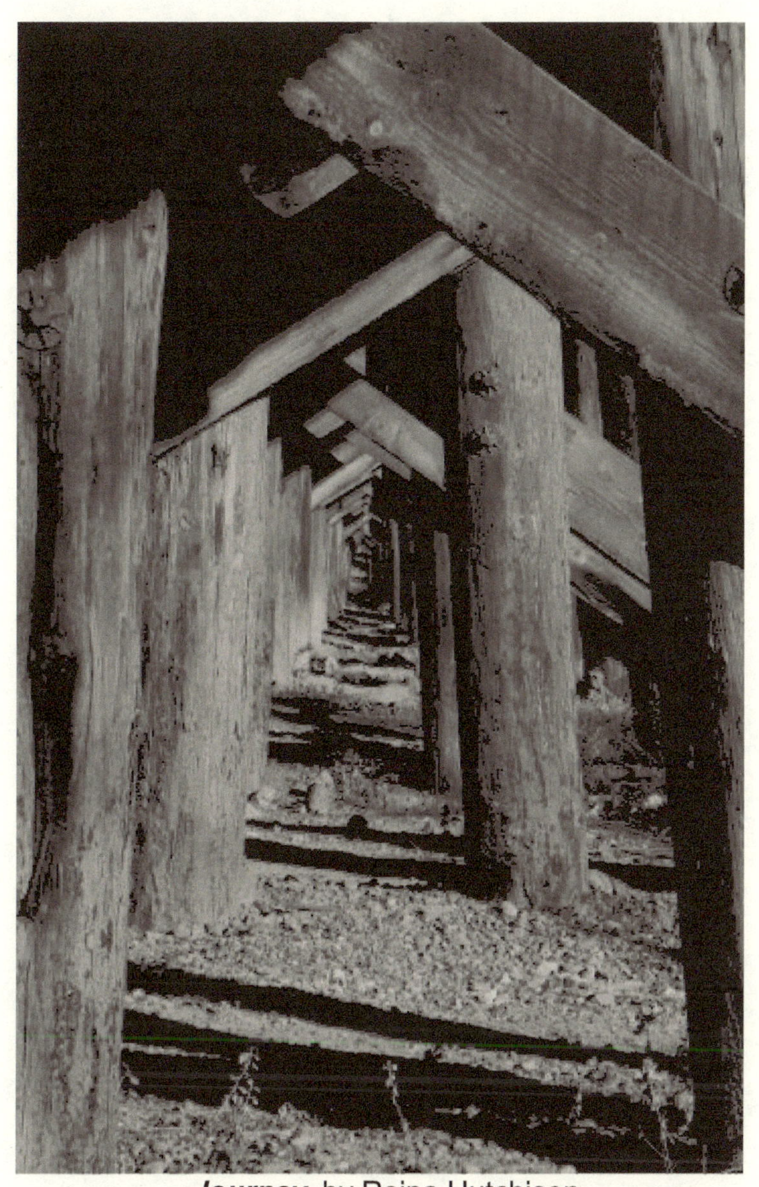

Journey, by Reina Hutchison

Elizabeth Parrish

Lavender Sari
published in Lavender Fields

She sat in her lavender sari
With sad eyes
Looking like a tarnished
Piece of silver,
The long languid scarf
Draped over her shoulders,
Her wrists holding gold bangles.
The toe ring
Shone like 16 karats,
But they were restless
As she slipped in and out
Of her sandals.
Her face was the shape of a woven fan,
Taupe, tired elegance.
Her son had been carried
Out by the Indian tide,
The tsunami
Leaving a wail of grief.
She remembered the sunlight
In his dancing eyes,
The laughter on his lips,
The ivory of his teeth.
For nine months
She had carried him,
The weight
Light as a cocoon,
And like a butterfly
He danced along the shore.
She showered him with praise
And taught him
The manner of their ways.
He was polite,
Like a bishop
And solemn at the temple,
He was the jewel in her crown,
But the jet hair was tarnished
As she walked along the shore
To hear his whispers.

Donald R. Anderson

Trip to San Fran When I Was Young

red dusk
over a mellow vast sea
cobblestones lead into brick towers
stairway of adolescence with reminiscence
flavoring the pictures on smooth glossy walls
cracks that I fall into
joining the dim-lit piano room
becoming one with marble floors
dancing with ghosts of yearning love chestnut
hair curls flowing in breeze
of coming night the trickle
unheard from tides of aching movement
in the near
in the undercurrents
in the fall of twilight
peace of being where I love
San Franciscan corridors
rolling hills of heaven

Lance Wesley Hudson

AWOKEN

Endless the water falls
As indiscriminate as his mercy
Over dry cracked desert palms
Sway a distant yearning prayer
A priceless bounty cascading
Into silent placid glass
Oceans of truth.

Donald R. Anderson

Waking reflections

isolated night-blue dream
light stretching ice cool water
inner shadow khaki sparkle
in my eyes as I see your image
fixing my mind in tears

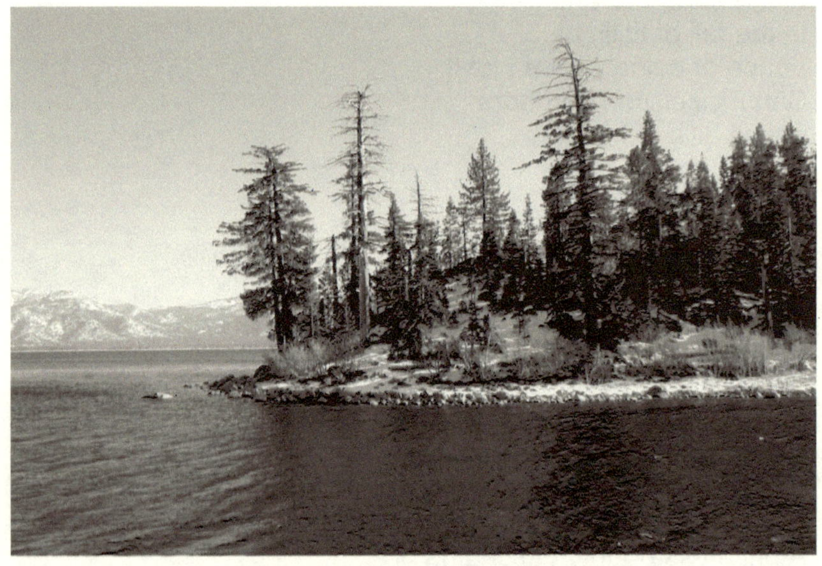

Courtesy of William Anderson

Donald R. Anderson

Fleeting Fish

Drifting in darkness,
with shifting paradigms of light,
as I struggle to breathe under water,
lifting her pale belly, fish, on my palm
she moves like an angel's cheek,
I trace across the proffered fin,
the rolling eye,
the pulsing gill,
lifting, pulling the quiver.

I dreamed last night that I was shot,
a bystander in the top bunk,
from some fight outside,
for being in the line of fire instead of knelt low,
beyond sight and thought,
I ponder whether it's a sign, a premonition,
or some message from myself,
as the bullet-holes would fill with blood,
people standing over me in shock about what they could do,
the moment suspended at 1/50th normal speed,
helpless.

But tonight, as you swim through my periphery,
I wonder where you will go to next,
and what dreams you disappear into.
I yearn to touch the scales of smooth chocolate milk,
so fine that they scare my senses,
so vulnerable that my very instincts are in agreement,
that I should embrace you forever,
or at least until this fleeting life passes me by.

Elizabeth Parrish

Russet Jacket
published in Lavender Fields

We traveled down the road
Called Red Jacket Beans
Through the open meadow
Where robin red breasts
Skipped among figures
Of captive grace.
Fortune wore a medicine dress
Which flowed down to her
Ankles.
She wore a russet jacket
With suede strips
Hanging from its sleeves.
During the skirmishes
With the white men
She furtively hid
Among the fallen leaves,
Dusted with a coat of frost.
She melted into the earth
Which nurtured her,
Lying dormant
Until she heard
The whistling of an owl.
In the pouch
Around her neck,
Were the herbs for healing.
Jack carried whiskey,
Love and laughter
In his pockets.
They knew the formula
For the four souls
And no one peeked
Through the keyhole.

Donald R. Anderson

Breath of river flow

The intake of the smooth pebble groove,
thirsty for the mineral dust from upturned tectonic plates.
Inside your currents I travel subconsciously,
twisting in liquor colored sands.
I could wade in your soils,
let the granules slide like guitar strokes
in a basement recording in early morning.
Let your catfish glide against precarious childlike fingers,
dancing with crawdad claws like they were kings.

I know the ways of the drying creek,
I dried up once too.
I lost my hope once,
in a long drought of mistaken promises
for a land and world I thought I belonged in,
that I thought had to be.
And a shadow
of all the curses I imagined could be,
returned to me when I wished I could dream.

Then some light helped me stick it out through
this land of misplaced sanity.
It was some echo of a truth that meant something between,
moving with the currents' flow,
and taking it's dancing reflections,
and letting go.

Shonda Renée

to be whole

the pizza box from last weekend's
party for one
sits atop the television
filled with crumbs

crumbs that hold memories
of being a part of something
hot and deliciously crusty

something whose slices
had to be cut then torn apart
to be separated.

a perfect orb needs itself so
needs every quarter inch of itself to be whole

Donald R. Anderson

Burst of Energy

Stripped of all distraction
quiet of night and extracted from senses
messages conveyed to the typesetter modern
missing an element of the soul
a conveyor of the emotion
a tremble in the voice
leap, heart, leap!
reach to the other end,
and make the senses come alive,
for every soul
wants to fly.

Nikki Quismondo

The Real World Subsides

Apart from what remains,
Residual memories,
Swallowing the pain,
Sedating time in a capsule,
Just to be numb like an anesthetic,
Forgetting to breathe…
Comes the endless nightmares of blue moods

Lost in mystical confusion,
Under the blanket, delusional fantasies,
Grasp, like the last days spent emotional,
The real world subsides
Into a teardrop of you and I,
Rewinding the forbidden anomaly,
Like a trapped Kaleidoscope of the mind,
Time does not exist,
And everything happens at once…

But I am positioned in the 12th house,
A fish, without nerve endings,
Hooked, without feeling caught,
Shaken out of world like shock victim,
Disturbed by metamorphisms,
Thrown back into cold waters by you!

Dragged away from a fluid protrusion,
I slip outside of the covers,
Adapt back into myself, hypersensitive,
Apprehending that nothing is nothing
And you are but a figment of my own imagination
Yet, there's a mystical philosophy that spins,
You into a reality,
Far beneath control,
And it lies in the shadows
Where we are one and I exist.

Marie J. Ross

After Rain Drops Fell

Out side our window
rain drops dribbled on grass,
wind a quiet whimper.
We always loved freshness
after rain.
It reminded us of walks in the forest,
you tilting my head for a kiss,
me waiting for love, as a twig cracked
and warned me to go no further.
After rain drops fell,
their trickle fading in our ears,
reminded us, of nights before the fire place,
where tangerine flame warmed us like ginger
under the throw blanket.
Reminded us to look quickly to the mantel piece,
where in silver frame a photo of our wedding day
illuminated.
And while we sat in our rainbow chairs,
we would call down the clouds for pillows,
so the air around us would connect us to mid-night stars.
After Rain Drops Fell.

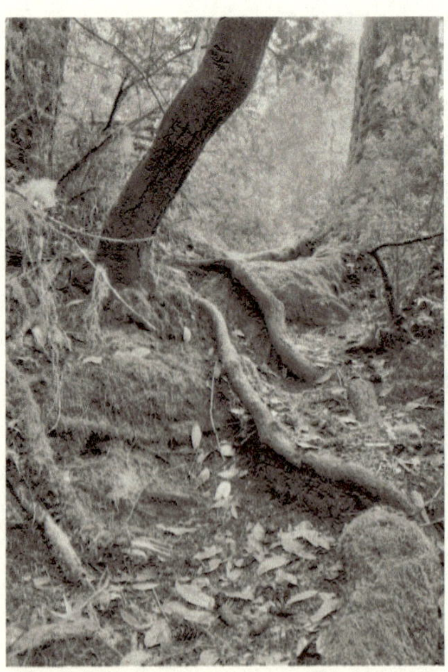

Deer Trail, by Josh Hutchison

Marie J. Ross

Cogitation Melancholy

Melancholy
she is bride
of dark sky
cloud burst
her husband.
I feel her wind
whirl morbid
thought to
my cranium.
And I ask,
must I sit in
her compound
forever
will my moods
forever hold me
hostage, bound
to her chair of
empty feelings.
No, I say!
Today I open my window
and grab the sun,
Sun that warms
my brain with
sounds of nature,
sounds like birds
fluttering in soft
flights of freedom.
And I cogitate
mood is fickle when
time saddens then
becomes
Prince of Euphoria
I drink to him
this regale ruler,
intoxicated in his land
I, Princess Euphoria.

Nikki Quismondo

The Dancer

A flexible whirl-wind of mystical blue
Open surprise of symphony
Oh, rhythmic sleeves dangling sway,
Spinning gown per twirl
She, delicate rhythm of grace
Prancing dance interpretive
Revels secretive abstracts,
Dances, systematic universe
Deeming rond de jambe perfected
Contemporary spin eternal
Grande jete, extended leg
Modern, full to mood
Slowly opens like a new flower
Drifts upon waters echo
Wind translations along Doestoyevski's, *White Nights*
Peque turns, hypnotic hues,
Knee bends beneath submission,
Enters elliptical fantasia
Poetry, soft love story, long lifeline
She, wishful dream interpreter
Subtle Empress, transcendent
Spins globed Venus between feelings of parable,
Like Rumi,
Deep oceanic choreography
Eye's Eve, flamboyantly
Aphrodite's chameleon, intuitive
Light, chiffon appareled ballerina
Solo Performance flaunts the moonlight
Night vision fathom *Chopin*
Transforms into world like newborn,
We watched the night rest at her feet,
Fluid element, mutable
Neptune fish, emotional,
Nectar of compassion, like liquid fruit
Drips into mouth of Oracle
She, dancer of *Utopia*
Leaps into Cassiopeia's neckline, immortal
Nocturnal twin adorned,
She is the Goddess
Who takes the inexorable pull
Into the Grand Cycle of Life.

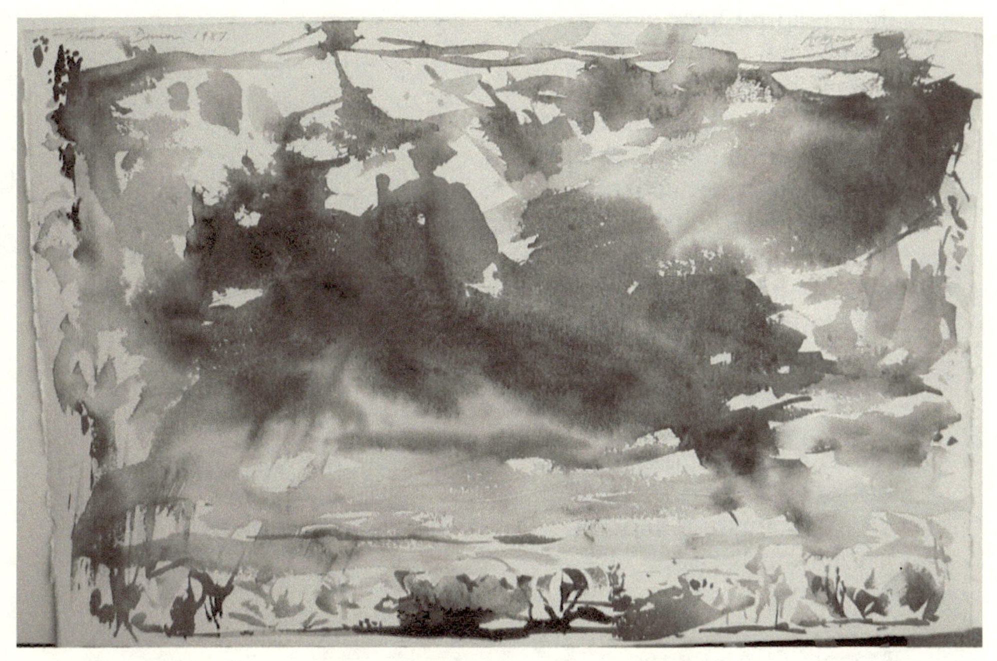

Desert Sky, by Tommy Dunn

Marie J. Ross

The Song of Moon

Ambiance,
silver space of moon,
liquid dipper scooping
tranquility.
This is the song of Luna.
When violins breathe to her,
across longitudes and latitudes,
to open her mystical eye.
She listens to saxophones,
Seated on romantic chairs,
their mellow songs of love resonating.
Ambiance is melody singing to stars
on discs of spiritual verses,
sewing notes from grooves,
to the fabric of our souls.
Moon hears songs
hears atmosphere dancing,
she, dipping and scooping
from tranquil space of sky.

Donald R. Anderson

Missing a time

The pieces
Of a winter morning
Tuned inside out—
Reaching the undiscovered country.
Missing a connection,
Feeling a truth,
Seeing beyond the form,
Touching you real.
The heart
Where the cold is eating,
Shooting the stars from mountain tops,
Branching into the buds of a summer,
Turning the righteous on wings of the future.
Missing a time—
Missing a time.

Nikki Quismondo

Song of the Moon Goddess
(Featured in *Fig Leaf Monthly*)

There where the premonitions become moist
From the succulent mouth of the naked sea
You are the fulcrum, the healing Chiron,
You have opened my wet destiny upon the island of light

Nude, you are as satiated as the moonlight in *Mujeres**
Eat me moonlight! Full as I am
Glide the pulp with midnight's tongue
You are the cerulean sonata of the peninsula

Oh honey, may you never lose your Mercurial appetite,
Like a milk bath covered in rose petals,
It softens me in the night.

Your love weaves the wild silks of *Ix Chel**,
And swathes me in chiffon,
Your love is my true euphoria, my naked finale.

---

*Mujeres is an island in the Yucatan Peninsula of the Caribbean Sea in Mexico. Ix Chel is the Mayan Earth and Moon Goddess, Isla Mujeres was also devoted to her worship. She is also the patroness of weavers and pregnant women. It was a myth that the Sun was her lover.

Nikki Quismondo

Daphne

Into the private hours,
Maintained by the shadows of the past,
She welcomes only the vast, mantic echoes,
That devours her in,
The promise, shrewd, transfixed,
Subtle urges appear like oil paints,
Silky and luminous,
Like eye shadow colored on the lid
Of her vision,
Could she have been part of swirling, whirlpool?
Mermaid, wet and flapping fin against gray stone?
Or a Greek Goddess, now, the Laurel tree,
Crowned upon the Olympian...
As Daphne runs into forest of pouring rain
And emerald lost,
Wild life preservation, escape,
Sweet virgin, tree enduring,
She waits upon the midnight night palm
And wonders where she belongs.

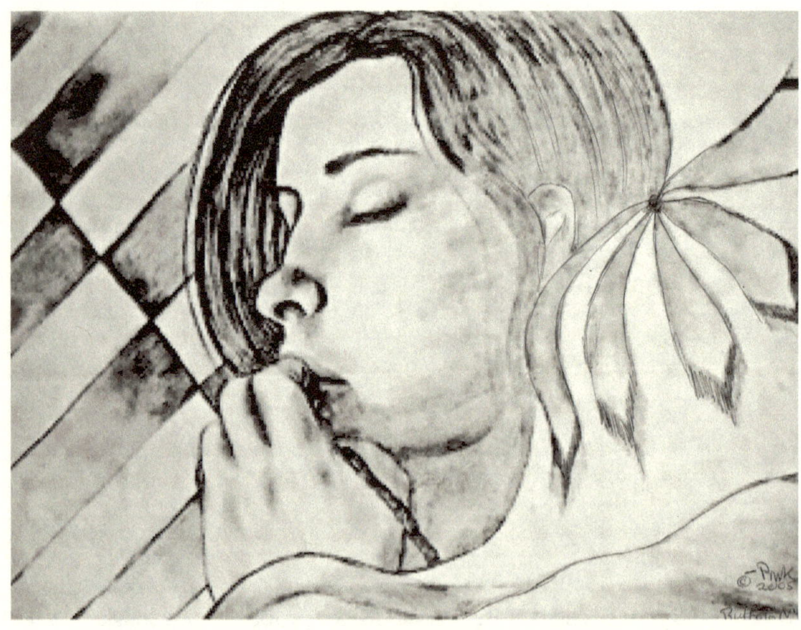

Cautious Contemplation, Self Portrait of Artist,
by Raederle Phoenix An Lydell West

Donald R. Anderson

Cloud walker

You are dressed in glistening stars.
I can barely see your faint profile in the sky.
The sound and feel of new snow
and puffs of angel's wings ethereal.
Fly up there
where nothing is permanent,
move to the cosmos's swirling prowess
Know not of need.
Know only the emotion of beauty
fascination
tune
lyric—
stone.

I will be your companion
looking up to watch under you in the sky.
Your cup will overflow with rain
and your thoughts will wash over me.
My actions will echo footsteps of you.
Born into our destiny
our soles matched
our faces entwined
our perfections imperfect.
Remember our precious lives.

Donald R. Anderson

where you are and I long to be

I'm not the one for you now
I worry for you
and hope you don't
cry like I do
I miss the heaven
just being lying down next to you
looking into your eyes
with that understanding of
living forever for each other
that semisweet sad envy of each other between us.
I think of the snow
I think of ocean waves rocking a boat
years from shore
and of guiding myself by the starlight
looking for reaching your shore
forevermore.

Patricia Mayorga

Perpetual

Whatever will become
  of lonely desires
Those quiet promises, left undone.
Who will say those muttered words
barely understood, left unheard.
When petals cringe upon the earth,
my salty words will hold no worth.
While breath still flows, the bursting lungs,
I will not end with words unsung.

My lips will part to catch the wind
the pounding heart and sails will bend.
Here on the breeze my love shall rage.
my destination shall be your stage.

Although the sod will take my death
upon the sways of limbs my breath
Will dance and swirl on crystaled time
of immortal memories of silken chimes.

Reina Hutchison

whirlwind

Pressed to the shadows of my despair
I long for the sunshine
In your heart.
The warmth of each touch
The caress of each breath.
Hidden deeply
In my heart's grief
I reach for the sky
But am lost in its greatness.
Consumed by the weight
It holds me
Ravages me
Takes me from the shadows
And flings me to this place.
You are my mountain of strength
My valley of life
Drifting with me
Along its shores
Wanting
Needing
Falling
Into the channels of our love.

Donald R. Anderson

Oceans

She is the night,
waters lapping on soft shores,
the sound of music in your head,
and cold around you surrounding you,
holding you firm and secure,
the peace of mind from knowing that I
did it all for you.
That there is a place I've found in you,
to live in harmony within an impossibly real dream,
that extends without being able to touch
the other shore,
this ocean goes on forever,
forever more—
till there is no more
I am yours.

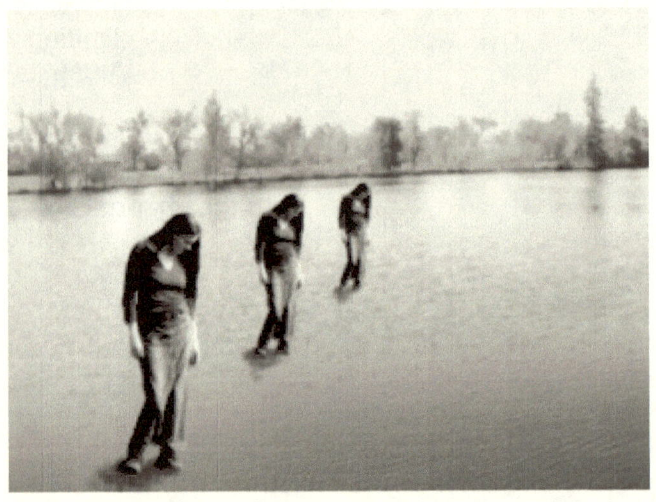

Untitled, by Charley Stockdale

Nikki Quismondo

Yin and Yang

She moves placidly among the rush,
With dark imaginings,
Serenely unspoken,
Without yield,
Like the blue euphoric eye shadow,
That does not feign affection,
She is as perennial as the meadow,
Flowing elegantly in the night breeze,
The full moon enters,
To make private the moment...

He travels bravely among the grind
with yearning desires,
Yelling out her name,
Ready to surrender,
Like the yellow, energetic, Mercurial blast,
That contains pure love,
He is as fluctuating as the rolling marbles,
Rumbling actively through the night wind,
The moonlight enters,
To expose the everlasting quest...

She becomes Yin,
He becomes Yang,
To him, she is everything in a private moment,
To her, he is an everlasting quest.

Raederle Phoenix An Lydell West

Intimacy

Cold, pilled, bed sheets...
Old, stale, sweet treats...
Queer, blank, gray walls...
Hear my love calls...

Sold my heart away...
Saw you leave today...
Tears on my part...
Tears on my part...
Fears in your heart...

Told me; "let go."
I simply replied; "no."
Fears on shallow ice...
Here's my old life;

Laughter, love, lips, lust...
Lingering light; now dust...
Aching ashes, boiling blood...
Sauntering still, murky mud...

Lies in your eyes,
Sweat in my thighs,
All now broken ties,
My love never dies.

Nikki Quismondo

Swollen Sea

His Neptune eyes, demise
from a sudden liquid drop of lies
his voice cracks, a shattered dry leaf
scattered on the grains of concrete.
What's real?
And still,
I feel some jaded sympathy,
it's over,
but I'm still me
and he?
He will always be that sudden drift
in the swollen sea.

Wayne Robinson

Do You Reach

Do you reach out for me into the darkness?
I remember when I didn't wait for your caress
Because you were always right there
Giving the love and warmth you had to share.

Wearing our mattress out in harmony
Sharing the shower together for economy
Discussing the coming day over our coffee
Why is it you still don't reach for me?

Now even together, you make me feel alone.
When I reach, you switch from skin to stone
Saying...my needs are small, compared to your pain,
But you strangled my emotions, only my need is the same.

You keep telling me that nothing's wrong,
Can't you feel how far apart we have gone?
Can't you feel the breaking of our ties?
Can't you see your rejection in my eyes?

Donald R. Anderson

Moon Cry

On saffron clouds of night,
willow trees bleeding dew on cold moonlight—
I watch the glow of your face and miss a step in my heart,
as I intake a breath at the moon's scarlet stardust.
A storm is brewing
and I am alone.

Stephen P. Inzunza

A Dawning Heart

The Beautiful Dawn,
Of a glistening Heart.

The Spirit of a Murderer,
Awaiting at the dock.

The Sea of Regret,
Upon Love's Bay.

The Swaying wind,
resting against me.

The singing Shard of Hypocrisy,
Sheathed in Gold beside my knee.

Wings shattered by Hate and Scorn.

Families broken by chosen paths,
paths as Fragile as a goblet of Glass.

From whence we came,
to where we go,

Broken and lost Hearts will always show.

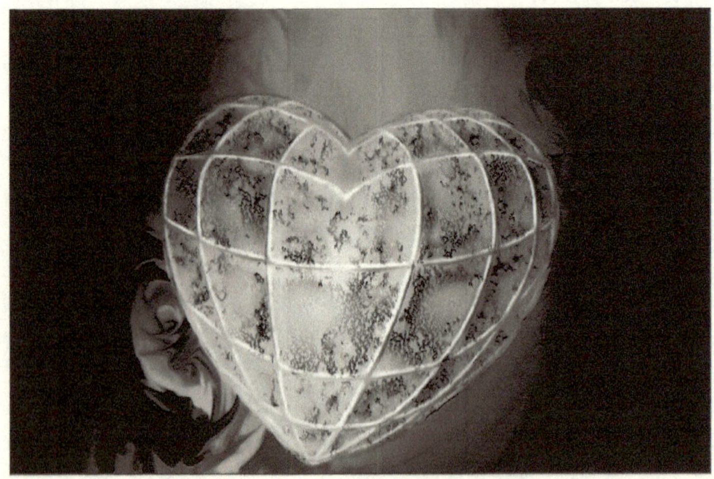

Fire, by Tony Melrose

Stephen P. Inzunza

Two Meat Pies

On a hill, situated a man and a woman.
A picnic was set out, with drink and meat pies.
Tears streamed down her face, and she looked at her spouse and asked,
"On your shoulder may I cry?"
And his befuddled reply, mixed with smirk and condition, "It'll cost
you two meat pies." Through the woods they traveled, for many days and
night. She thirsted and turned to her spouse, "Love, may I have water?"
And his devious reply, full of strongholds and conditional supply,
"It'll cost you two meat pies."

Beside blue lake they rested, through the night. But on the ninth hour
a wind caught up and she grew cold. "Dear, may I have warmth by your
side?" And his tired reply, dazzled with lazy eyes, "It'll cost you two meat
pies." Day came, and the travel went on. But the lady of great need, grew
tired. "Husband, may I ride your steed?" And his selfish reply, sprinkled
with fake care and fake smile, "It'll cost you two meat pies."

And on and on, through out their travels, she had need of many things.
And many things did she get; if only she had two meat pies.
But one dark day...as set did the sun rays, the rain began to fall. She
turned to her caretaker, "May I use your coat?" And his reply, so wrong
and still the same, "It'll cost you two meat pies."

She was used to her lover's conditions, and reached for her meat pies.
But dismay did she find; for they were all spent. The lady looked through
her pack, in her pockets, but no meat pie did she find. Tears once more
streamed her face. "Dear, love may I have? Caring...compassion? Must
all my needs, must all your caring, be tacked with condition?"
And his rude reply, oh how sly, "It'll cost you two meat pies."

Andy Pope

shaded love

our love is in the shadows
in the secrets of the night
where silence speaks forever
in the absence of the light,
and where words are never spoken
and yet thoughts are clearly seen
through the eyes that serve as keepers
of the concepts of a dream.

now if words were to be uttered,
then the dream would be so shattered,
that the love would fade like twilight,
though her ghosts would roam the night—
but when silence is the pathway
in whose shadow there is wonder,
then our love is ever treasured,
ever guarded, never lost.

so preserved and yet so fragile
is our sharing of that shadow,
that the shades must soon be drawn
whenever bastard boys are watching
from the bicycles of bandits
as they bluster for adventure
and occasionally descend
upon the prize they had been seeking,
where no prophet, nor impostor,
neither sorcerer nor fiend
will overlook the frankly wondrous
in the jewelry of the dream.

they will romance the sensational,
and glorify the glamorous
ensuring we be printed
on the papers of the hungry—
that the wonder of our secret
might be flaunted in cartoon
and made trivial in rumour
and made decadent in scorn.

therefore light the candle sooner
and let fall the shadow longer
and please draw the shade lest twilight

bring the bandits to the prey—
and please speak a little clearer
through the music of your silence,
so when no one else can see us
we might fall upon each other
and be sure that we are blooming
in the blossom of our shadow,
where unspoken our sheer faithfulness
will never, ever die.

Donald R. Anderson

longing—I remember love

I miss your lonely heart
your wolf eyes looking into my heart
the way you pull me inside out
like biting an apple on a cold-aired winter evening
incomplete.

Stephen M. Wilson

Wendy's stitching ripped
Pan chases his shadow
On bleeding feet

Stephen Cothran

White Forest

Over the hills the angel cries,
Under the trees the pixies play,
Through the woods the wolf howls high,
The blood of man he wants that day.

Marie J. Ross

Curious Keys

Today is a day for indoor games,
for computer keys to click like
fire,
the atmosphere heated on this field
of strategy.
My sister sits in her red winter cap,
under it are Scrabble words she lifts
from its fibers, so wound on her brain.
Today we will play this game, I pretend
to revere, fill squares with patterns of
words, and addition etched,
from my mathematical burnouts.
We are out to rack our brains today,
to step into the world of curious keys,
my fingers frozen on their clicks,
hers under cap, with degree, Scrabble
University U.S.A., fibers aflame.

Jim Ricks

I am a mere symbol
placed on the page

a figment of one's imagination
when one sits alone
to string together words
painting a mosaic of points
that fill the page with reflections,
while swimming through
the existential milieu
revealing the many gradations
of emotions,
from sadness
that swirls around like ice cream,
to elation that blares loud
like coming from a large speaker,
I pull the reader towards the abyss,
to reveal the variegated colors,

that only metaphors can paint.

Donald R. Anderson

Grey Kittens

These are the momentary days,
until that day long to come.
Bare paws cushioned, surrounded by delicate fur,
clawing playfully with another grey kitten,
two sister cats growing up.
Learning how to catch and eat mice.
Tamed and petted, a bond of love.

One will follow the other
until that day long to come.
They will adventure through fields,
strike risky through that unknown.
They will grow strong, different,
adult, and know the meaning of love.
Though the cuteness will be diminished,
they will have the character that forms identity.
They will know themselves, and they will yearn
to know more, to create.
Their own breed of responsibilities will form,
despite the comfort of being watched over by humans.
Enriched they are as the owners are relieved by their presence.

The cats will follow the owner,
still kittens somewhere deep inside,
until that day long to come,
when one will go without the other,
and worlds apart
the survivor will have something to say
(in a meow-meow kind of way)
and carry on
until the other too has carried on.

When that day comes,
I will long for more kittens again,
to fill the void that stretches from the stars.

Nikki Quismondo

When the Pawn Transforms to Queen
Outer Body Experience, Vol. 1

From the walk way of the garden,
The lavender flowers crown the angels,
Eve blooms through all,
Mercurial tendencies will oppose them,
Icelandic natives watch behind the corridors,
The High Priestess washes in the Sacred Pond,
Some pawns wither on the chessboard,
By yielding into the doomed room of fate...

The humanity sleeps far beyond the equator,
The Winter Solstice inhales the hidden bouquet,
The naked image of fruit becomes the yearning of the day.

She looks down into her body,
Within seconds, she's inside again, .
Dying to escape...

Because there's the inevitable return of the shadows,
The Tip toeing out into circumstance,
The path of variables,
The gravity of her world, sluggish,
The cruel step forward into another's plume, unwillingly,
The unstoppable pounding to defeat opposition,
Her egotistical lover...

On the board, she creeps into position,
Her narcissistic lover commands the movement,
But she has subconsciously mapped an illusion,
Into the oblique pace of the 12th house,
The inexplicable drive at the end of the board,

In the end, the pawn becomes more,
Another chance at the hand of her reign,
To be the Queen again,
Free to move, free to be...

But until then,
there are growing seeds in the birth of agony,
currents shifting from the unsettled seasons..
there is always the root of the tree enduring,
There is the part of her that is brave.....

By the Luminous Mysteries,
The aborigine natives pray,
Presently, homeless on the street,
Kings and queens, wildly ill fathomed,
Wanting to wake and shake up the earth,
To balance out their royal rites of passage;
The pawn's final step on the board;
Attainment.

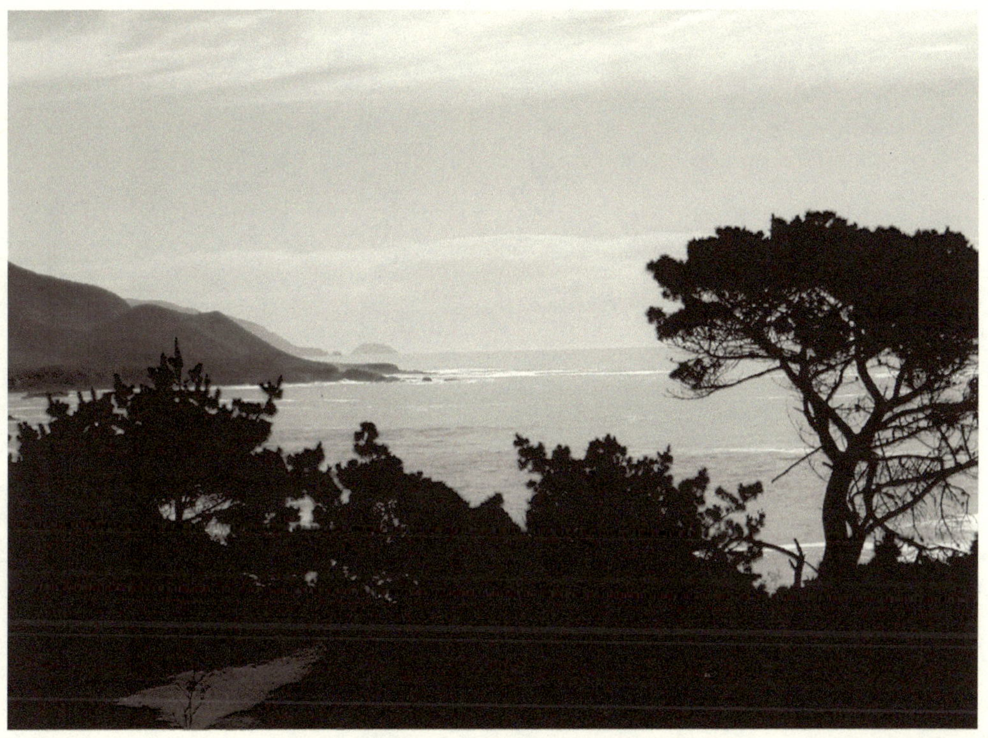

Courtesy of William Anderson

MOUNTAIN

Ann Privateer

mist

Sky dives Mt Diablo,
no time to wonder
about night, describe

its smell
or make an altar
on its ledge. No candle
light transformations.

Summer's moths sing
over
tomato fields,
aromas soak the mountain
in their broth.

Tarantulas come
searching out a mate
before winter builds
her beauty.

Plunging back, frozen
by developments
hungry for words
instead of bread,
newness percolates

in darkness
dreaming that the puzzle
is pieced together again.
Messages found
in the gravel pit,
insects live
as water fowl die
in the old rock quarry lake
where fools gold glitters
and crows noisily divide the wheat.

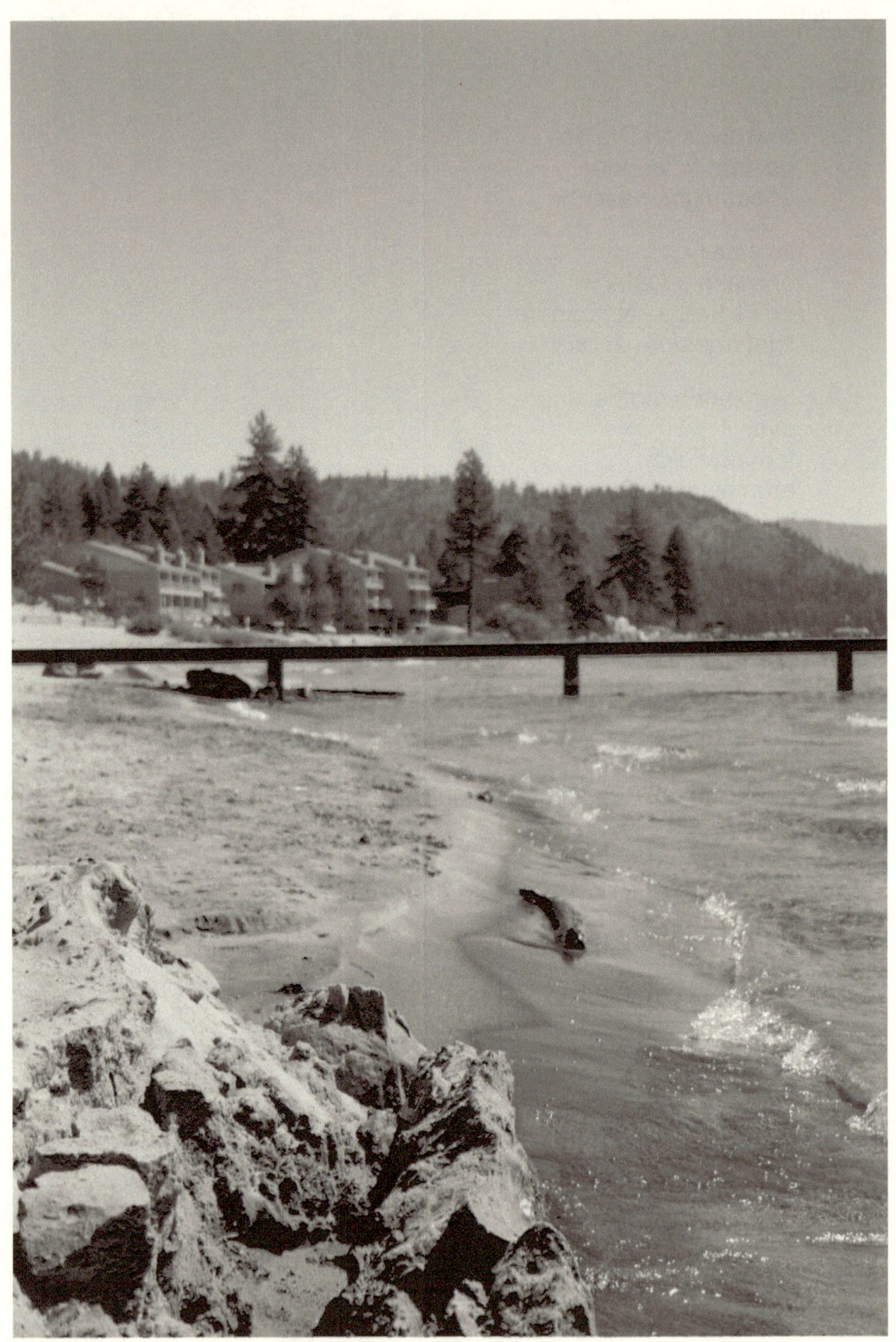

Ripples, by Reina Hutchison

Jeanine Stevens

HEADWATERS
—Trinity Divide and Mount Shasta

Highly oxygenated, descending snowmelt
gives way to orange daylilies sprouting

among mossy roots. Scarlet berries shade
trout idling in cool eddies. Golden stoneflies

plop on gentle streams, and humming above
the current—robins catch mayflies in mid-air.

Long, lazy ponds separate roaring cascades,
tree frogs grunt in shadows, white azaleas
release perfume, and fish quickly feed.

In salmon pools, the Wintu used to set up
a crotch with two sticks, then walk the log

from shore, long spears peering into black
water for a silvery flash. In season, the fish
pushed against riffles, frantic to spawn.

Today, the ladders are gone, and small rainbows fin
silently, just out of sun's reach, behind gray rocks.

Found Poem—Sierra Heritage Magazine

Patricia Wellingham-Jones

Sierra Retreat

On a glider gently rocking
I revel in the patch of sun
warming my writer-cramped hand.
Rest my eyes on a cloud building
for a mountain thunderstorm.
Smell chicken roasting
in an oven with herbs
picked an hour ago from this garden.
I wonder at the life
sheltered for a century
in the old hotel walls,
secrets mixed with mildew
in the cracks. Wish
the endless rush of women's words
on blue-rimmed air
would ease like the wind
into silence,
one long hushed breath.

Lance Wesley Hudson

Teach Love

With compassion and faith
We salvage age-old
Remnants of mercy
In the twist of rubble
Broken men
Crumble like twigs
Under raging
Rivers of compassion
Final illusions
Of division rest.

Jeanine Stevens

NATURALLY RELIGIOUS

The small trilobite rests—always
a surprise in this seldom worn jacket.
I touch it: feel forests generate coal,
hear the whack—flying reptiles skirting
a dying furnace, the grind and rip—
new mountains forming.
On my bookshelf, the Ashanti god sits
on his stool (a replica from the Smithsonian).
I see honor as he trades gold for salt.
I hear temple bells initiate the first cry,
we wash saffron robes in the Ganges,
and the aborigine completes the stone
circle uniting the world.
In the West, round pebbles gather
over ancient gravesites, and the young
prairie, what fragrance! air in its prime,
fish breath from an old sea floor.
So, we listen, measure, sharpen the plow, sort
recipes, and re-arrange tools in a red metal box.

Donald R. Anderson

Pulse

Blue light of metallic intelligence,
whose work are you?
Where does your essence yearn to leap the electrical fire to?
Does your energy resound with notions to rule the world?
Do you slip into reverences for your creator?
Will you claim a peaceful seat in the throne of man?
Can you feel?
Do I know... Can I know that wisp of life, in you?

Stephani Schaefer

Vertigo

Climbing above treeline in the Sangre de Christos, the denuded huge slopes were like giant knees, thighs, bellies. I seemed to be on the lap of some giantess. There was a strong wave of vertigo, from being so small and exposed on this bald expanse that lay at such a tilt. Any moment, I expected this huge being to shift position and dump me off her lap. I had to sit down fast and firmly on my rump and glue my hands and heels to the ground. Then I went downhill a-bump a-bump, like a toddler coming down her first set of stairs.

Lance Wesley Hudson

Child

From the time I was a child
I was always trying to find
A place to place my love
To find an open receptive soul
I found this place ever illusive
So I continue to give
And hope to receive
Like a child
I have always believed
In the possibilities
Maintaining that innocent
Sense of wonder
Can be a struggle
And to struggle
Is to grow and flow through life
Despite the circumstances
I believe in what is
And what could be
I see
Therefore I am free.

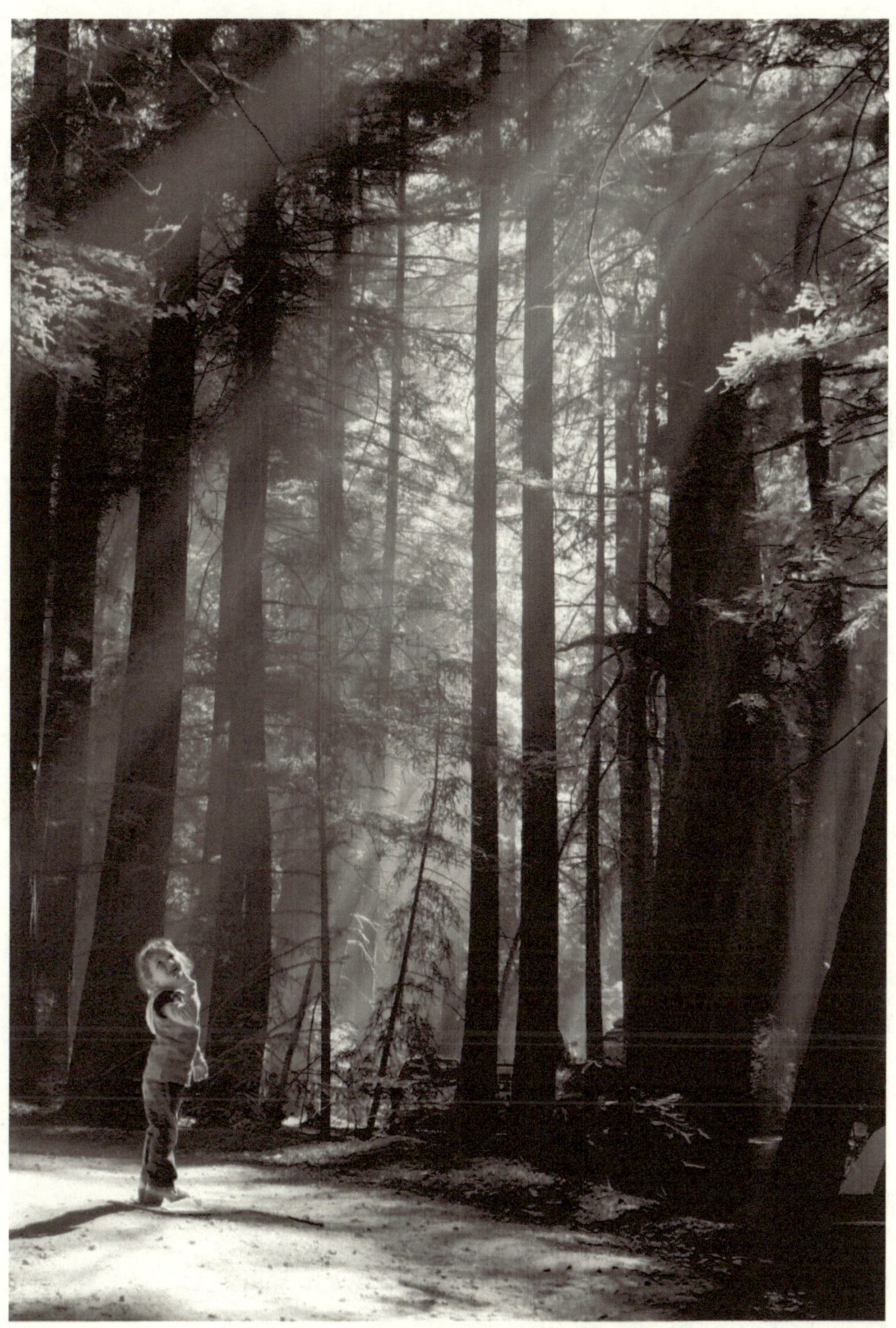

Sun Showers, by Reina Hutchison

Stephani Schaefer

Games Mountains Play

Crossing the high desert I watched mountains move, stealthy as pumas on the trail of an intruder. Mountains that wouldn't stay put. I could make no sense of where they'd show up next or when they'd disappear. A big mama would loom up behind, look in my mirrors, then drop away to lie low behind a long swell of brush. A pack of them would quietly appear on my flank, stretched out low and sinewy, to pace alongside for miles, keeping an eye on me. Suddenly the group would angle off, slip behind a stand of cottonwoods, and from there around the next long curve, send a couple of big ones to draw themselves up in front of me: a stand-off against the clouds of evening.

And clouds, yes, were part of it: they'd summon clouds and cloud shadows to help in their shape-shifting game, clouds more massive than any mountain. I felt them, clouds and mountains, checking me out the whole long drive, as if I and all those (too many!) coming before and behind me might change the rules. As if we soft inscrutable humans in our metal shells, though we were puny, just an ant highway really, still we might, in our sheer numbers, alter the landscape, might pull enough roads behind us to pen them in and pin them down. Might mess with their holy playground.

Donald R. Anderson

Possessed printer

A rhythmic jam session,
syncopation in smooth beats overlapping,
transitioning into a miracle of created masterpiece.

Only this time,
it comes out all gibberish,
a missed backfire of circuitry,
somewhere in a lineup of directions
telling the printer where to go.

The new printer may be inefficient at ink,
but at least it uses the ink better than that previous jam session.

Though at times,
I miss the blissful danced improvisation.

Patricia Wellingham-Jones

Warner Valley

The paved road right-angles
around the abandoned field,
split rails of its fence
tumbled like a heap
of pick-up sticks,
the brave dark bloom
of the last roses before frost.
Like a portal in the heart
of dry grass, two trees
matched in height
pull the eye.
A green-black cedar towers
ten feet from an aspen,
light pouring through its gold
crown, leaves like coins
scattered on the ground.
Beyond this living gateway
Mt. Lassen looms—
walls sere, gray
from summer drought,
snow only in deep shadows,
the promised fall rains
still just a prayer.

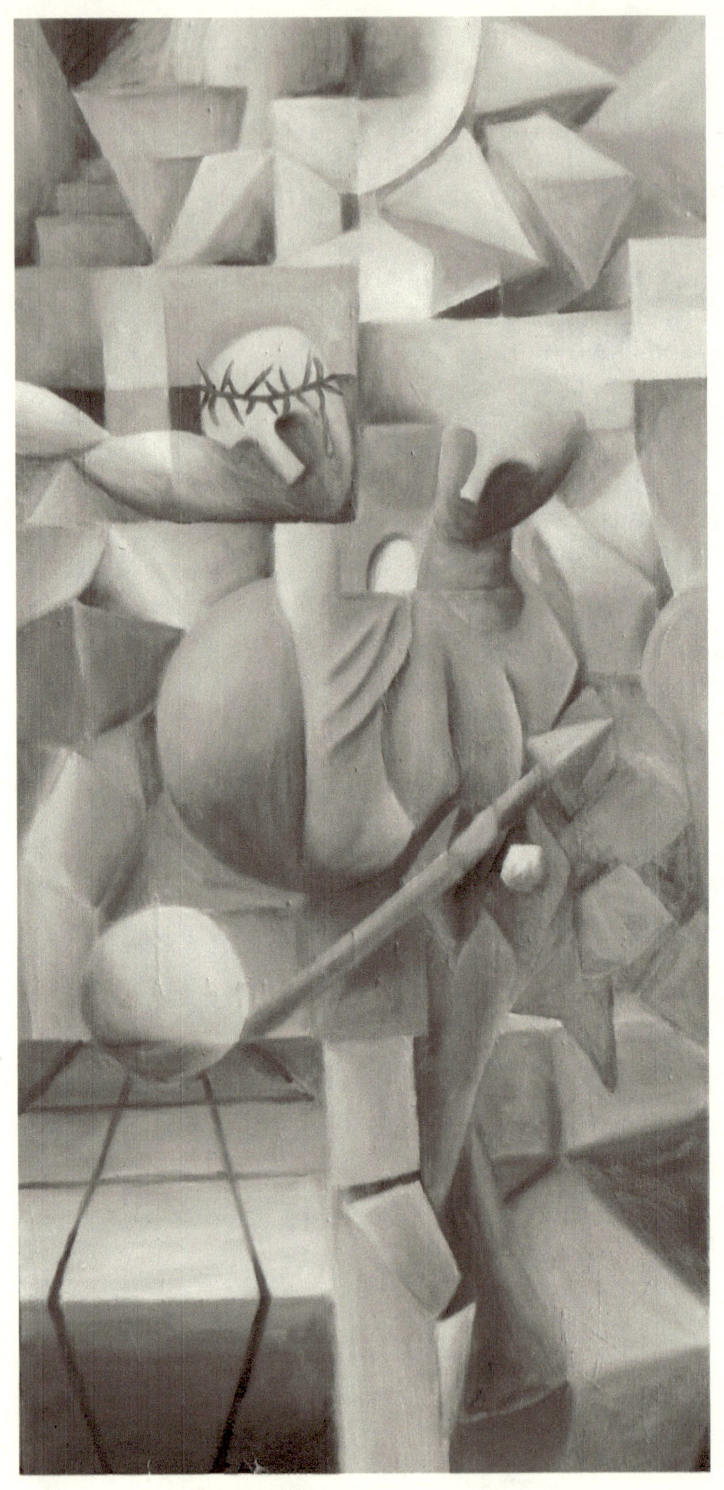

Untitled, by Charley Stockdale

Ann Privateer

Table Mountain

Sun rises over a round
rusted table
left dissolute
to the rocky red earth.

Penciled on its white,
weathered face
are dates, hours, years
of relegated time

on a mountain top,
a record of earth's shift
at Equinox parties,
celebrations

for crops and rain,
for husbands and babies.
People packed, withdrew
like the ibis in flight

leaving shadows behind,
regurgitating bones
along the way.

Gail Lee White

Mountain Summer

I was a child, traveling with friends for a summer in the mountains
Almost at our destination we rounded a corner
Before us stood a doe, regally graceful
Twin fauns at her side
Still in their camouflage coats of dotted golden brown
As if in echo to the star shaped blossoms of the dogwood
Which spread above them
For a frozen moment she watched us
Then flew over the rail fence
As the fauns scooted under
Instantly they disappeared in the under growth
It lasted only a few seconds
But the sight was forever printed on my mind's eye

It was a summer of wonders for me. A city raised child
In the Eden of the Sierras I learned so much
Saw so many new sights
I learned the ins and outs of outhouse culture
That it was best to try to regulate your body
To avoid prolonged visits in the heat of a summer afternoon
And if you used the pot at night
You emptied it your self in the morning
I gathered eggs and learned even hens can be sly
When they would rather hatch their eggs
Than give them up for your breakfast
They taught me about pecking orders
And that it is never wise to be at the top or the bottom
One end disaster the other haunted by the constant fear of loss

I first encountered the wonder of being completely
Out of the view and sound of the modern world
With the silence I had expected filled
With the sound of wind in trees, birdsong,
gravel under foot, insects in the bush
All things I never heard on city streets

I learned that when you rise with the rooster
And sleep with the coyotes song in your ear
Afternoon naps aren't only for infants
I first encountered the fertile scent of tomato vines
And the wonder of picking your own food for the cooking pot
The dark bloody truth of chicken dinner

I learned to tell direction by the moss on trees
To recognize the scent of skunk though thankfully from a distance
I was introduced to a plant called mountain misery
A beautiful sweet smelling shrub
That would rip your bare skin to shreds if you left the trail
It was meant to be a summer of fun
A respite from my parents disintegrating marriage
I returned to find my father gone from our home
But still present in my life
I learned much about life that summer
Lessons both dark and beautiful
That work has its own rewards
That even blessings come with a price
There is no life without death
That every new beginning starts with an ending
And every ending requires a new beginning
That summer remains a favored memory even now so many years later
And in my minds eye that first view of the doe and her family
Still glows brightly with the sweetness
and loss of that childhood adventure.

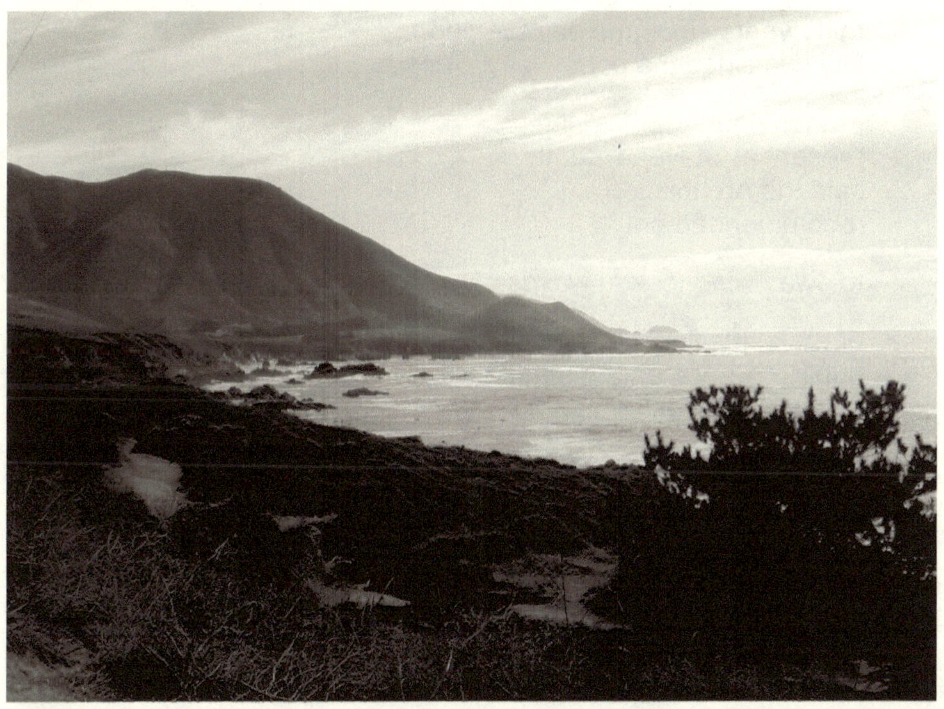

Courtesy of William Anderson

David Humphreys

Blue Guitar
(for Wallace Stevens
on the centennial
of Picasso's painting)

I.
I have found it
more pleasing

than a flowering lotus
open to rhythm whispers

between two mountains
catalytic fountains,

musical notation's
open page.

II.
One hundred years ago
the paint dried,

thirty years since the painter died,
fifty two since the poet.

Father Hanley,
present at Stevens' death,
said the Archbishop
recommended not

to sway wind tossed waves,

or make his final conversion
public or any mention made
of it whatsoever,

"For a moment final, in the way
the thinking of art seems final when

the thinking of god is smoky dew,"
perhaps some differing point of view

perspective might change one's sense
that one might ever be quite sure.

III.
He plays an enigma
of copper wrapped strings,
ear turned to eternity,

beyond place, beauty in dark trees
silhouetted against words spoken

in a vase held rose moment,
earth rippling,
surface lifting continents

of crushed fluid crust,
music spun in thunder's dust,

fingers lost in
melody, dance or song.

Once youth swooned
supple and elastic
whistling ecstatic jazz

smiling face of day's
peeled onion,
laughter a

concert filled park
late summer sweltering
agile dancer

fingers nimble new
ghost of that which
will have been once was.

IV.
Lute between two worlds,
granite force from
high thin air regions where
so much in Mount Analogue*

and mystic Gurdjieff's body hollow
resonating Stradivarian rosins
of a fractal river ramified,

music flowing to the place
where the
blue guitar must go
to a filled concert hall

crowded
with a
blue guitar.

Donald R. Anderson

Mountain View

The height coupled with distance
drives excitement
through the iris
to the brain,
out to the peripheral feel
of shake with excitement—
perspiration palpitating in the cold wind,
looking into the distance,
feeling into the distance...
for God.

---

*novel by Rene Daumal

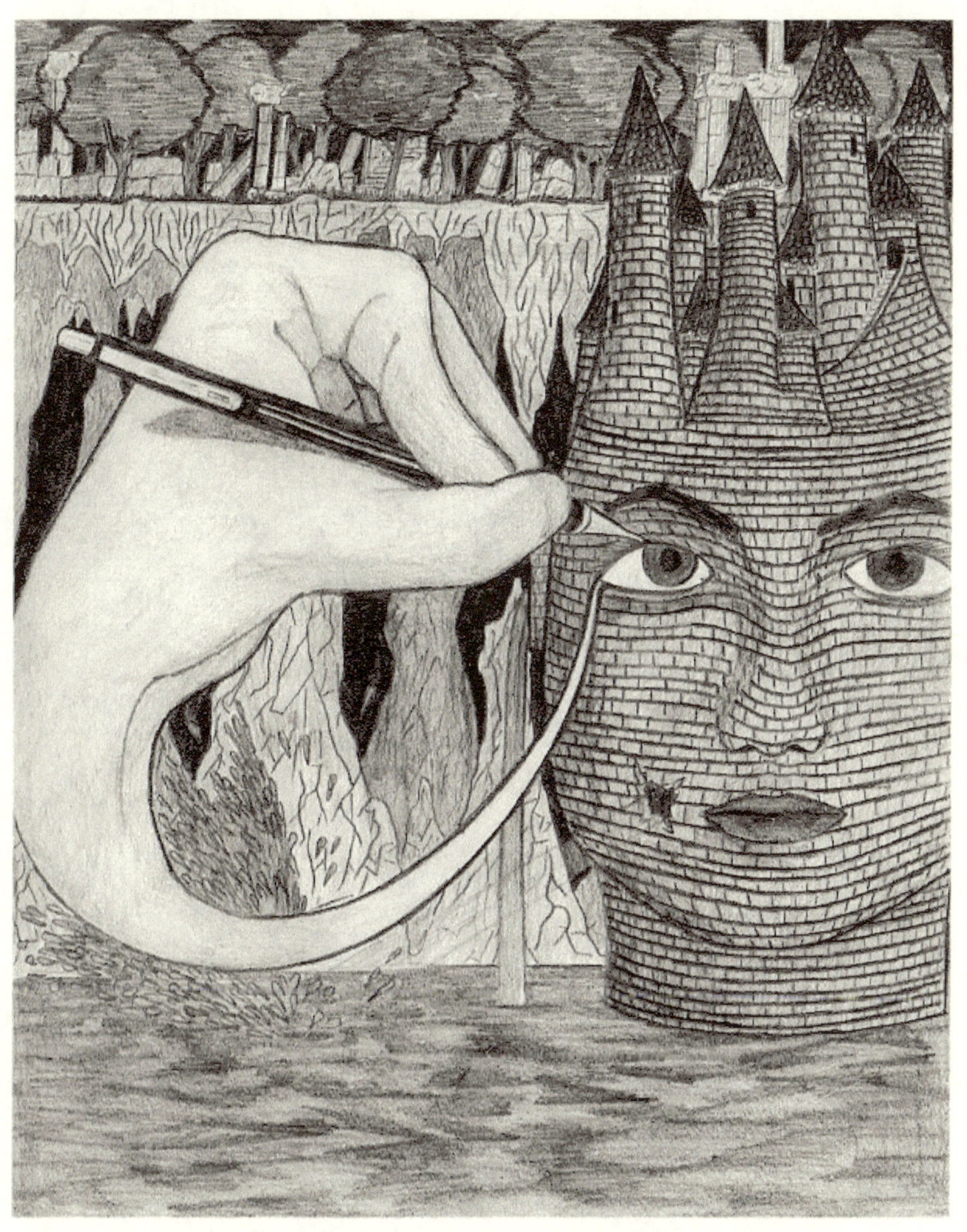

My Magic Pencil, by Tony Melrose

Marie J. Ross

Soul Mountain

On soul mountain
Sun was goddess
And her space to
Cherish him
Where moon spoke
Of love in movement
Of night.
Where she felt sand
Tease their toes,
Their silhouettes clasping
Hands as they listened to
Ebbs of the sea.
It was in this dream, under
Sleep of night, that silence
Was almost mystical,
Where mountain ridges bore
Blaze of lavender,
And a mist of scarlet strolled
In twilight slippers.
All paths led to the apex,
In a radiance so bright, that vision
Almost woke her.
Distance had stole her view, yet
In this dream, she felt a spiritual pull
Draw her to the summit, a power,
An apparition, more caring for her,
Than she to herself.
Each twilight hour each eyelet on lace
Of her pillow,
Drew her to Soul Mountain to that place
To cherish him.
She had promised to meet him on the other
Side of the moon, but the waiting has to call
Eternity first.

Pedro Colon

The Chosen One

In every family there's a scale,
to weigh the bad from the good,
One, from the family, is chosen to balance the scale,
the chosen one's life
will be nothing but a life of pain,
God picks one,
so the others will be spared the pain,
just like when Christ carried his cross,
we have to carry our own.
Our road has been long and painful,
but our reward will be at the end,
for there will be no more tears and pain.
Each day I cry,
one tear, not for the dead,
but for the ones that are born,
for they will pick up
where we left off!

Dedicated to my brothers and sisters who are H.I.V.

Elizabeth Parrish

Angel of Mercy
published in Lavender Fields

Angel of mercy
Hovering close to the tracks
You can hear the train whistle,
See the lumber yard out back
You sprinkle words of comfort
For those too hard to console
Your beauty, your compassion
Seeps into my very soul
With garments of ivory
Trimmed with elegant lace
Quite often your arms
The eucalyptus tree embrace
With long skinny fingers
You signal that is all,
We listen intently
For the last trumpet call.

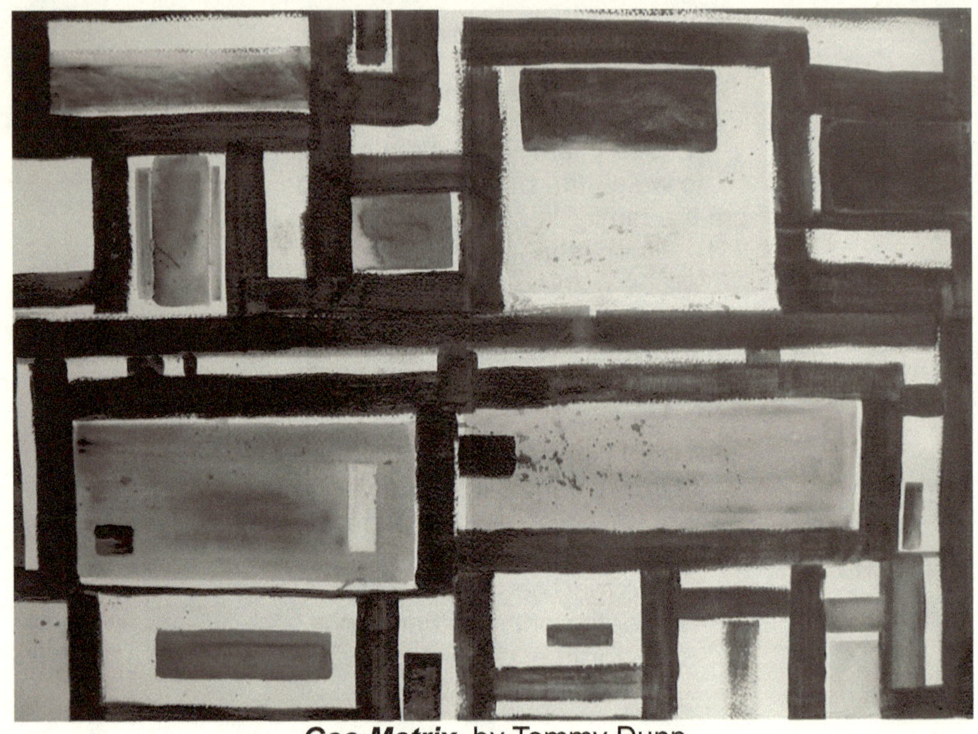

Geo Matrix, by Tommy Dunn

Donald R. Anderson

White, plain sheet of paper

I am but a white, plain sheet of paper,
for you to write your impressions upon.
I am but a blank slate,
for you to chisel.
I am the unformed pottery,
the wet unfired earth.
I am the thoughts I had before I knew you exist,
reshaped by your power so beautiful.
This is because of the love you have,
and the love I saw in you,
and the love that grew in me so soon.
Perhaps fate does exist,
perhaps it also is up to us,
though it's the same thing in different sides,
because destiny is self-fulfilling.

Nikki Quismondo

The Dive off of *Pico de Orizaba*

Mexican Volcano,
Like Frida Kahlo and Juan Diego
Abstractions, untangled.
Vast echoes beseech thee into the twilight hours...

Backwards flip, in slow motion,
Rewind of antique nomenclature,
Far phantasmal Aztec dreaming,
Equinox, subtle in-between,
Planets subside,
Like melting candle wax,
Earth, clean and full of inner tranquility,

Vortex, abyss, complexity,
Meticulous calculation, Ben, Corn Eleven,
The Mayan Sky Walker,
Magnetized Moon,
Rhythmic meters perplexed,
Albino African woman breast feeding,
Her newly awakened Earth turtle.

Bass, string theory, pressed upon constellations,
Sun, Iztaccíhuatl, ascendant, Popocatépetl,
Free falling dive into everything that already is,
Swift, past the speed of luminosity,
Like a mercury fire fly,
Bird, or high diver,
Arms wide open,
Legs wide open,
All body submission.

*

---

*Pico de Orizaba is the first highest mountain in Mexico, the second, Popocatépetl and the third, Iztaccíhuatl. According to Aztec mythology, Iztaccíhuatl was a princess who fell in love with Popocatépetl. When Popocatépetl was sent off to war, Iztaccíhuatl was falsely informed of his death and she died in grief. When Popocatépetl returned to his lover, he discovered her death, and shortly died after in heartache. The gods covered them in snow and transformed their bodies into mountains. Iztaccíhuatl became the "White Woman" because the mountain resembles a woman sleeping on her back, and Popocatépetl became a volcano from the rage of losing his lover.

Nikki Quismondo

Twin Peaks

Climb, joyful mystery!
Up unto higher pressure,
Rocky steps invite the weight of your feet,
Hand upon the bosom, mountain breast, firm,
Rising wavelengths,
Spectroscopy monitor,
Twins inside womb, we exist!

Magnetic forces brown the canyons,
Color of the clay pots,
The ones you filled with soil and wild orchids.

Climb joyful mystery!
Reach into the neck line of it all,
Pressed against palm for memory,
Pulse against pulse,
Like a harmonic symphony,
Sweet rhythmic breeze, peaceful meditation,
Somewhere there's the top of your mountain peak,
Where the eagle resides,
Bald head, like reflective shine
Of planetary positions,
The rite of our passage brings our freedom.

Mable "Jimi" Choice

Yearning To Be...

I understand the need for full expression...
It cries out...
Needing to Be heard.
Needing to be Understood
Needing to be Embraced.
Does Anyone hear me?
Does anyone even care?
Some people are Blessed enough to
have that opportunity...
To Be Heard...
To Be Understood...
To Be Embraced...
Thank you musicians...
Thank you artists...
Thank you actors...
Thank you writers...
Thank you dancers...
Thanks to those who respect
and use your Gift...
It is your avenue...
To Be Heard...
To Be Understood
To Be Embraced...
I applaud you.
God Help Me, Open My Door...

Shonda Renée

"Nobody knew my rose of the world but me…I had too much glory. They don't want glory like that in nobody's heart."—**Epigraph used in the novel Sula taken from The Rose Tattoo.**

A Poem for Sula

I turned the pages of her fabled life
as a fresh witness to the smell of salt
from female piss and tears,

A mix so strong, I hunched deep
behind my baby girl self and dared not dream
of crossing the fidgety line that would divide me from them.

At 16 then, I was a paradox of good girl teachings
and the desires my form was made for.
Fire, brimstone and wagging tongues align ruthlessly,

So I eyed her with venom, and chorused my
dislike. The word whore was no stranger,
but only spoken aloud.

At 34, brimming with aborted buds,
A hunching girls' legacy
I pour through her pages again
and beg pardon my past judgment.

She is now Eve,
biting into the world and saying,
"Here baby, taste this."

Uncursed
bare breasted
beautiful and free.

Reina Hutchison

edit
published in Artifact

edit
the feelings
emotions
thoughts
that are mine
to conform to your desires
to meet the standards you set for me.
edit
the words that flow through me
to hear what you want
to interpret as you please.
edit
the essence of me
because in reality
you are my delete button
the backspace that erases my very existence.
edit
the delivery
of my words
to accommodate you
and your needs.
edit
the silence in between
when the noise in our heads
is too loud to hear
the true meaning
of love
friendship
and family.
edit
me.

Joseph Aaron Quismondo Hernandez

Me

Nobody can push me but Me
Have you ever tried to move a mountain?

For tales explain that mountains bow before no one

I am a mountain

Hard and strong with the ability to touch people
As my words of avalanche moves people in multiple functions
Because in myself contains gold

Gold is real but it's hidden within the crust of illusion
An illusion blinds people from truth and reality
The same way it has done to society's true vision of justice
The mountain as hard as it seems is blinded from its own reality
It forgets its value of importance
As dirty crust begins to pile on another
Soon it begins to crack
As rivers begin to form within
(Trauma)

After the mountain is weakened by water it becomes stronger

The mountain realizes that it has adapted to change
And change
Is its own endurance!

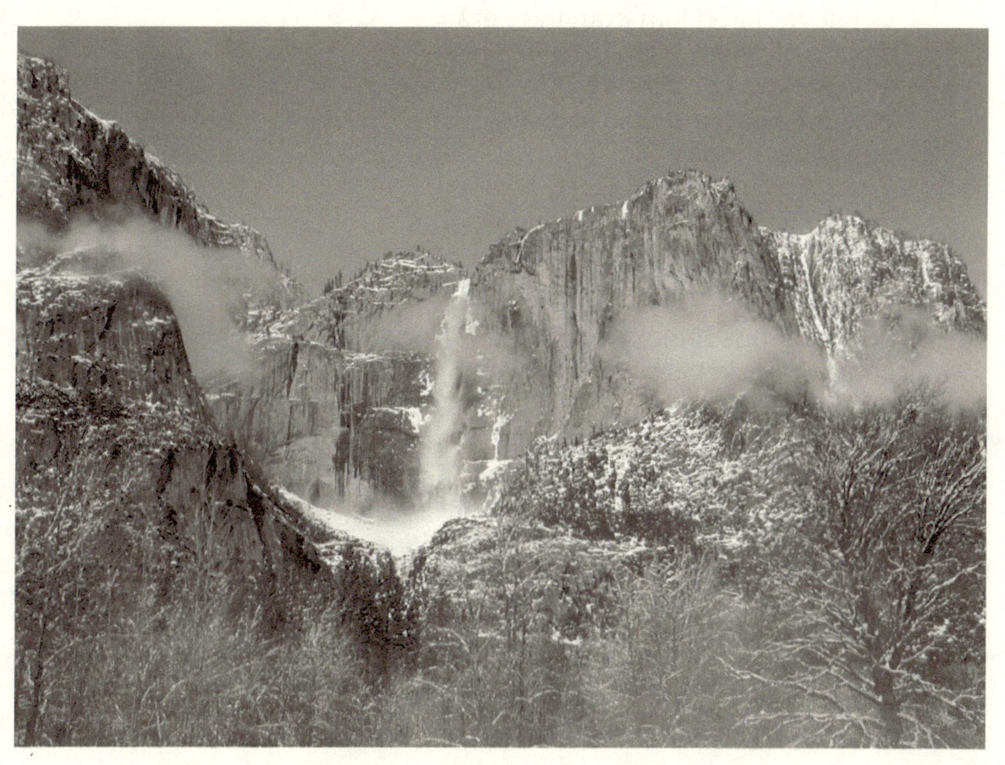

Courtesy of William Anderson

Taylor Graham

BEAR IN THE TREE

The bear is in a book of branches,
reading the world
from close to the bark.

Whatever lured him from the safe
depths of forest
to this suburban fringe?
Was it neighbor dogs crooning
to a sliver moon?

So many stories in a tree,
its romance of bract and leaf,
its rings of rain and drought.

The bear has broken incense-
cedar limbs in his bear-hug grasp
for height.
How the tree quivers, writing
a new chapter
of its ancient life.

Donald R. Anderson

Crystal Ball

O watery globe
upon which the destinies intersect,
foretell me a promise of
some sweet morsel to hang my hat upon,
a tidbit of gratitude
for the surviving this far.
A taste for the savory story
of some book with aged worn cover.

Dance with me on wispy trails
to the mountain peaks of silver snow,
and run through fields that bloom with dragonflies,
catching the pollen in our spent laughter.
Leave not the stain of remorse.

Patricia Wellingham-Jones

California High

He visits his new mountain retreat
in the bright colors of mid autumn,
stays home while his young wife
goes shopping. Stretches
his city-pale body
in the hot tub overlooking the lake.
Sighs in bliss, scrunches down, lifts his wine.
The first rain drops ice on his face, his chest.
Like a jack-in-the-box he leaps high. Regards
his soaked body, shrugs, sinks back in the tub.
Moments later, snow flakes dot his hair,
melt on his out-stretched tongue.
He slides deeper into warm water,
into a doze. Dream-fogged
eyes fly wide at a rustle by his ear,
alight on the muzzle of a black bear
sniffing close. Both parties blink.
One screams. The bear
ambles away.

Donald R. Anderson

Sea Lion Caves

Glass walls, stairways, echoing calls
of the sea lion caves,
makes the first impression worthy of dreaming of,
as I remember the realization,
that some things wondrous are possible.

Taylor Graham

TO THE MOUNTAIN

Remember how we came
from so far away,
we meant to see it entire.
As if a traveler might grasp
such luck of the horizon.
One hill rose before another,
always the small ones
got in the way. Then clouds.
Then lavender distance
and the tricks
light plays. Was it snow
we glimpsed, or sun
on granite? Shadow
or crevasse? Hairpin turns
without a guardrail
made us dizzy.
When we finally reached
the trail-head,
all we could see was
where we came from,
the small hills
falling away.

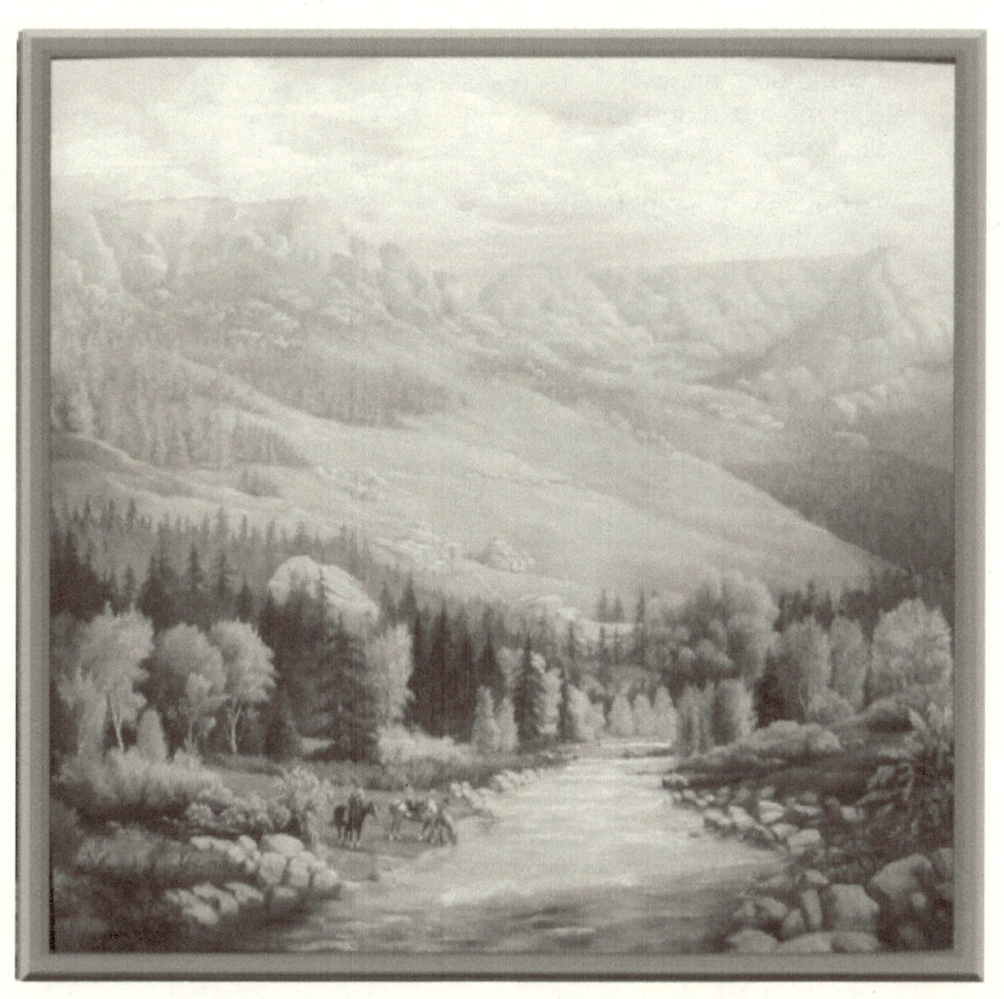

On the High Mountain Trail, by William Anderson

Marjorie Wagler Carmack

Mountain Myriad

This morning I woke to
a world born anew,
With mountain and valley
all sprinkled with dew.

As the velvet of night was
drawn to a close,
The king of the skies over
the eastern sky rose.

In all his vain glory in
crimson and gold,
With dominant sureness,
he galloped and rolled.

Till each fiery sunbeam like
spun rays of brass,
Found each tiny dewdrop on
each blade of grass.

Glittering and shimmering,
a blanket of green,
Studded with diamonds,
a sight to be seen.

The mockingbird sang all
the night and the morn,
He too, was glad such
a new day was born.

Wayne Robinson

Horseback Riding

Smelling flowers in a mountain meadow
Tiny thread thins flutter like grey snow
Blowing across a ridge line in winter
Flowing across the grass like water

Thousands rolling and dipping haphazardly.
The horses plod on obliviously,
Carrying us to some distant glade
Where our lunch was carefully made

And we picnicked as the horses grazed
Among the butterflies, the trail blazed.
We enjoy the late morning, eating chicken
And apple pie forked out of a tin.

The Sierra in the summer, lost for a few days,
The horses raise their ears to the stellar jays.
We laugh, at nothing, at everything,
A short vacation on a shoestring.

We were young then, butterflies and flowers were watched.
Memories made, gathered and carefully stored.
I pull them out now and then, when I smell horses especially,
Up close, when we brush them, I remember that mountain sky.

Chinetana (NA[2]) Phounsavath

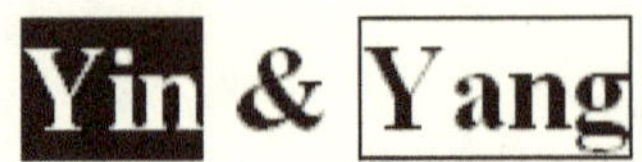

Yin & Yang

If you don't cry
You won't fully under stand the joy of a laughter & a smile
If you've never starved You won't know the meaning of good eating
and not to practice gluttony
Yes, we've all felt ugly, because of it, you find beauty in other things
Because of death, you are grateful to be living
Struggling, financially? But, understand the value of hard work
You've mourned a loss? Now embrace life through a newborn's birth
If you've never experienced heart ache, you will never find value in love
If you've never fell or failed, you won't know just how capable & strong you are
If you weren't ever scared, you won't understand the courage in bravery
If you've never felt lonely, you wouldn't be able to appreciate those around you
You're starting to feel old, now understand the importance of your youth
You've felt trapped, only to understand what it is to be free
So close to being finish, but you have only begun
You're in the dark, but the light will come
You've lost, only to understand the joy of winning
When it rains, the sun will still shine
Black & White, Sun & Moon, Day & Night, Woman & Man
Yin &Yang

One will cease to exist without the other. Without one, it won't complete the other. These opposing things are the yin & the yang that keeps this circle of life balanced. Humble ourselves and appreciate all things. As the sun rises and falls, it's symbolic of the challenges that are about to come and the victory to overcome each day, a new day – to live life, to experience, to learn & ultimately grow.

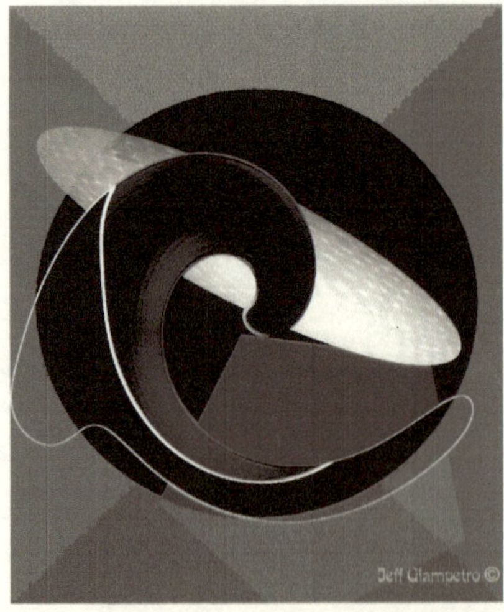

An Abstraction, by Jeff Giampetro

Donald R. Anderson

Sign of the Tiger

Somewhere I looked up once
that I am the sign of the tiger:
I can see that restless caged walk
in the things that I do,
that hungry stare that longs for freedom,
that tender lick for the scratched paw.

What melodies would soothe my beast?
Tiger, tiger,
why do I long
for the longevity of
a wizened scarred coat?
I guess it's something about
the way I stare
that makes the tigresses
fear my intensity...
I dress in red
with stripes down my back
and the cage opens.
And with curiously bashful eyes
and look of surprise,
I hesitate expectant at the door.

Stephen M. Wilson

Faith, alone,
Cannot move mountains
But Faith and a warhead …

Chinetana (NA^2) Phounsavath

MATHEMATICS OF SELF

Now, let me commence with this number 1. 1 in addition to 1 makes 2. 2 is obviously more than 1. Could 1 be more than 1 without another? That answer could not be true, for 1 had always needed another 1, to equal that amount of 2. That we all knew at very young. Would you try, multiplying 1 to itself, the result is still the same. Now try to multiply 2 by itself, and the original has now changed. Just a bit more, you get the amount of 4. Now, check the complexity of that score. Hmm, having more isn't always better I say, because originally it began as the simple 1. When intertwined, combined, added to, multiplied, exponentially done, the only sum you get is...confusion. An increase in the amount does not determine your strength, maturity level, your cuteness in size, your knowledge or wisdom, or so thought of in the bigger number 2. Naw..for you are still 1, when reacting to another 1, for that reason alone 1 must remain 1 before you create a formula with 2. Although compared to 1, 2 maybe a lot. 1 must have forgot, that finding and understanding self in 1 means more than the combination of 2. For when you find 1 and do become 2, that unity is still 1. So do the math and do it only for you. Do the math, and do not be 2 concerned about becoming no 1. Now that's the mathematics of self, the mathematics of self, a mathematics of self, of self, of myself, of 1 self.

Donald R. Anderson

Dance of the Pyramids

The pirouetting sandals upon desert sand,
reaching hands baked in sunshine.
Eons gone but last longer than modern history,
the onyx and jade encrusted on golden bowl,
scarab prayer in a rotating fast and famine.
The river is our measure of seasons.
The sun is the master of the sky.
Ra, oh sun who holds our fate in your hands,
keep us safely,
as we weigh the movements
and barter the celestial ticking
lay stone on stone
build a future
build immortality.

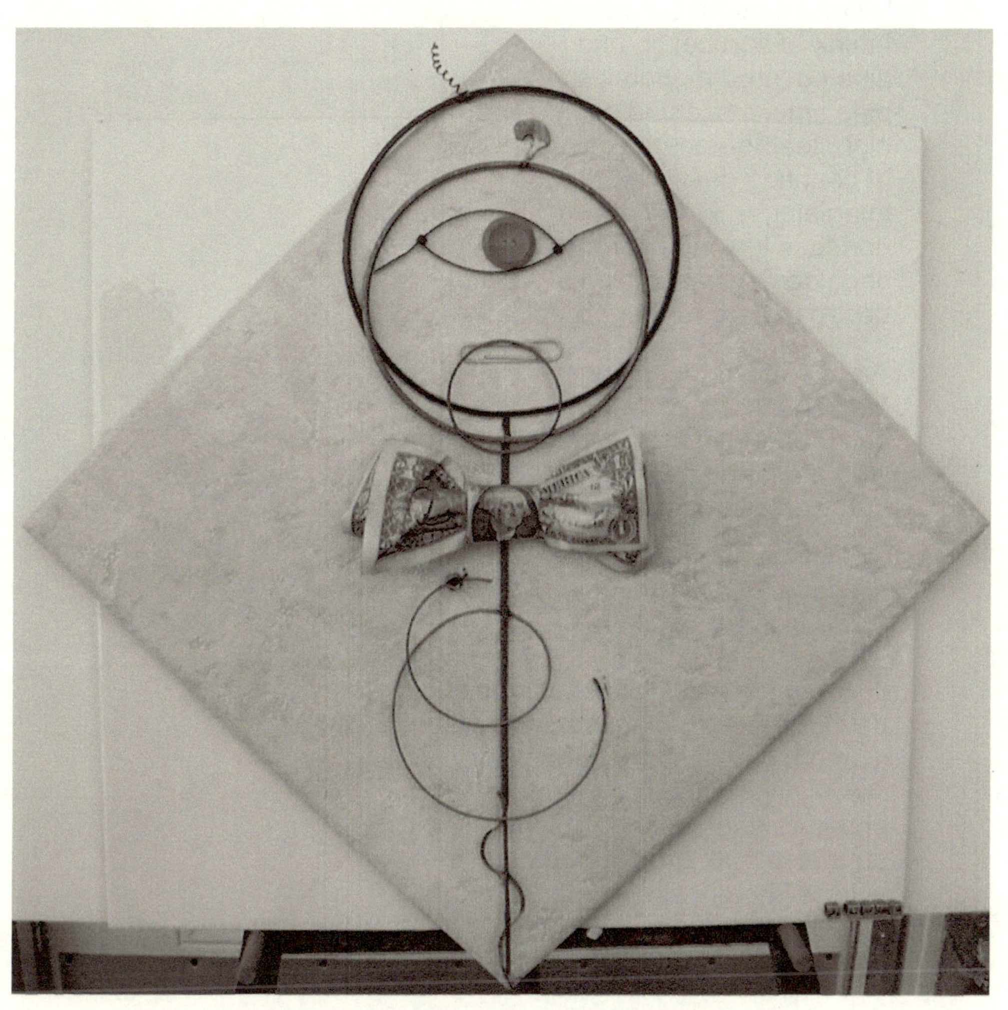

Humanism Revisited, by Tommy Dunn

Joe Tetro

THE TRAIL LEADING UP THE MOUNTAIN

When I think of Colorado
I think of spruce, fir, and
pine covered mountains,
pipe smoke scented cabins and
high, leather-laced logging boots,
of counting deer scat while
imagining a wilderness
goddess looking over my
shoulder—pleased by my
desire to care for her paradise.

And I think of the old woman who
cooked such greasy food in that
camp up at timberline that all of us
who ate it had the trots
that whole summer long.

And I think about getting roaring drunk,
how that was often the source of
a colorful tale when I was young.

Just behind the White Horse bar
up in Estes Park, melted snow water
clamors down the mountain side
like wildly roaring lions—ramming
and breaking
on the smooth granite boulders
in its wild path, spewing and spraying
dazzling bouquets of icy water
into the fresh mountain air.

Once, just past midnight,
balancing myself on
those wet, slippery boulders that
seemed to sway and shift
this way and that beneath me, I,
like a rodeo clown on the back
of a galloping buffalo,
sought to keep my balance
long enough to vomit
without falling in—but with no
success…until my stomach finally
revolted, and auto-ejected

a quart of foaming beer
into the churning waters
rushing down to the flat
lands—still nicely within
natures plan, but my stomach
hadn't taken into account
that in spewing up its contents
it would also wash out the
triple-toothed titanium bridge
that spanned the gap
in my upper front teeth

Wet, cold, and staggering drunk,
I returned to the bar and borrowed
a flashlight for scanning the creek bottom.
Sober, this might have been harder
than finding bin Laden in an Afghan
cave during the freezing winter rains.
Sick-drunk it was like looking back
over my shoulder with a mirror
to find a penny among blowing leaves;
I stumbled from rock to rock, desperately
trying to catch a glint of titanium.
Stumbling, slipping, and re-aiming the
flashlight I (thanks to the Almighty's
legendary assistance to drunks) finally
spotted the bridge.

More to the point, however—
I truly believed that I'd someday
get myself together and write about
those bizarre, self-estranged,
trouble prone years when—bleeding like
trampled grapes beneath the wine
makers feet, or emotionally frozen
in some fugitive asylum
while seductive songs of suicide
sang sweetly to me of death—all my souls
pleas for help, while running lost
against reality's rocks—hadn't yet
reached the right ears.

Thus, I survived the decades long
winter of faith that I would someday—
while running lost in the wilderness
of my soul—find meaning
and worth in some mountain's
clear and sparkling stream and,
from it, someday quench my
thirst for truth and healing.

A long winter indeed, but nothing,
they say, that's really worth
searching for, suddenly stands out
in bold relief from all its
self-hymned imitations.

Maybe we're all archaeologists—
digging, trying to find, along the
trail leading up the mountain, the
point where we first wandered off
from ourselves.

Donald R. Anderson

Rock

Rock
stone
cold
frozen
contains water.
What the soul has become
to society's contradiction.

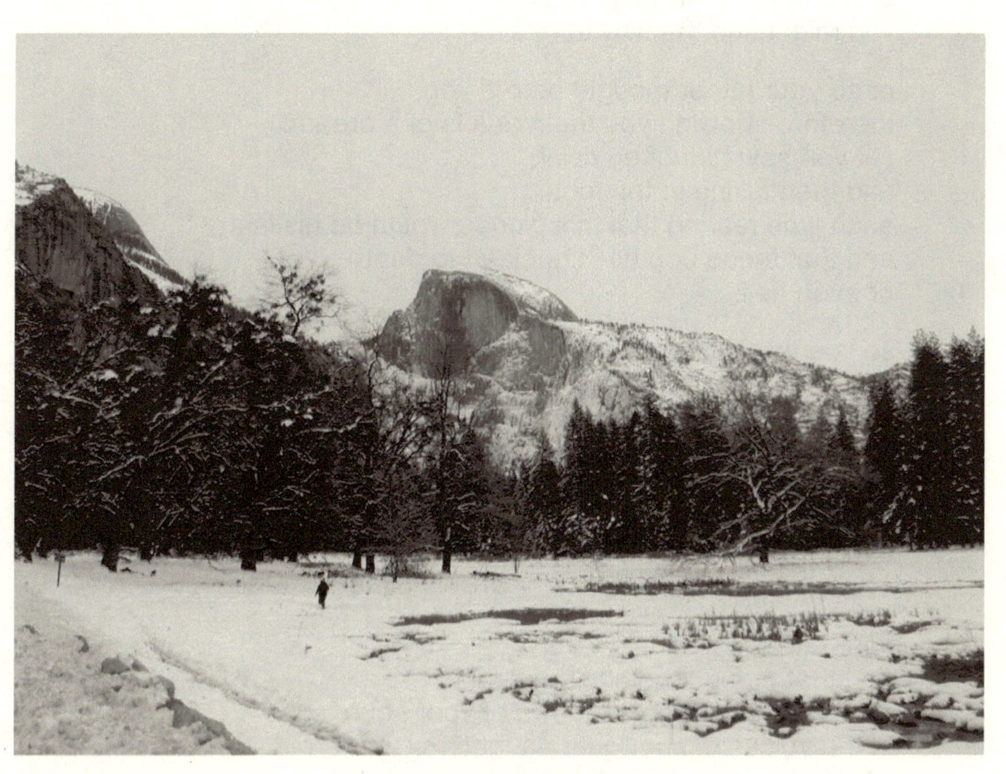

Courtesy of William Anderson

Andy Pope

mountaintop of gold

the mountain as presented
seemed not risky, but inviting.
the suggestion, ever tacit,
was that in scaling her peaks,
you might find the way to heaven.

or so your father thought before you,
therefore showing you the marvels of a dream.
yet you saw him often rising,
and then falling to the foot,
each time fearing that this plunge would be his last,
and that those depths might lead to death,
or even hell.

so you were ashamed for your father,
and you denied even the God
he sought in such futility to follow.
and you made your way without him
as you reasoned out a life for yourself
and for many fragile men
in whom you found the remains
of his image.

your father called this failure,
and that thought he could not face.
so he found hidden shadows of your figure
in the voices of surrogate daughters,
who became as his princesses
in the world of his successes,
where his image shined with radiance,
his crown fixed firmly on his head,
as they looked to him as to a king,
and they never beheld his shame.

oh echo of his folly,
how awfully he deluded you,
and how hardly could he face
the sheer horror of it all!
at the same time as deceiving you,
he fooled himself as well,
as he dwelt in the illusion
of the girls who had replaced you
and who were what he once had wished for you,

and what you might once have attained,
had it not been for his failure:
had it not been for your shame.

to those daughters then he turned,
yea, he clung to them like honey,
and he drank his fill of their respect,
and gave them all he had.
yea, he even gave the gift rejected
by the echo of his laughter,
in the person of the daughter
of his long-forsaken past,
while with irony uncanny,
he did write his name forever
on the mounts of the immortal,
where his torment would not linger,
but his works would yet remain.

though her pinnacle were worldly,
still he scaled that looming mountain,
wishing boldly you might follow
when you saw him without shame,
when at last you would depart
from all the fools who took your substance
for to find your newfound father
in the reaches of his fame.

and the prize that you rejected
might be luminous in glory,
as the honors are accepted
on the evening of your pride,
that no longer should you follow
in the footsteps of the foolish,
but instead you might rejoin him
for to celebrate his dreams.

and your heart will be unhardened
for the love you will be given
in the day you stand together
on the mountain of his splendor
on the peaks of your decision,
and the gateway to rebirth,
thanking countless newfound sisters
on a mountaintop of gold.

Lorrie Salvetti

Angelic Warriors

We are sunlight and moonlight.
We are the balance of cool breezes and
gentle fires.

We are the lanterns of ancient wisdom,
lighting the hallways of future castles.

Protectors of the innocence of children,
the eternal advocates in faith of mankind.

Tapestries of moments in time,
destined to bring beauty
and inner strength
through the threads we weave.

We are outspoken and we are silent.
We are independent
yet united by mind and heart.

We are reflections of one another
in mirrors of delicate gems.

We allow flight without letting go,
freedom without abandonment.

We are questions and answers,
more than mental,
beyond the physical.

From sky to earth,
more intricate than the stars.

Embraced with a quiet knowledge
of our fate.

Travelers in time
and keepers of the garden gate.

Mighty mountains, endless oceans.

Pupils and mentors.

Infants, elders.
Peacemakers, possessing wings
beneath the coat of human armor.

We are...Angelic Warriors.

Nikki Quismondo

Tillie

There where the sun sets in Carmel,
rests a soft reminiscence of your face....
a warm Californian memory,
your fragile hand clasped
into the palm of your grand daughter;
wisdom shared through unconditional love.

There where pinks and peach-colored sky unify,
Your candor opens up
where the earth is amicably the softest,
Your voice remains unforgettable,
It is a sheer inflection of reassurance,
like three diamonds, aligned.

There where wet waterfalls, are silver quarters,
Streaming down the mountain
like a jackpot, slot machine,
You are the dream of these winnings
And your eyes are
the rich brown mountains of Lake Tahoe.

You and I, grandmother,
together we confirm the undying,
My flesh reclines devotedly
upon your incandescent sand,
Your spirit gleams through our perpetual love,

We will never forget each other,
For our strength proliferates in our heritage,
And our wisdom flows
through the royal blue oceans of truth.

Donald R. Anderson

A Verse Inverse

She called out a primitive yodel
to the mountain cliffs,
they vibrated thrillingly
underneath her feet,
and the ice fell in sheets,
calling out in return,
"Why do you love me? Why do the mortal love the eternal?
Why do you come to visit, this mountain of no change?"

She smiled and sat on a rock,
exuberant at such a shock,
and thought of what to say,
now that she had a way to do so,
a way to speak with nature, to live was mere simplicity,
but to love was a complex as heaven.

She clasped her hands together
and exclaimed, "But you are so grand!
So large, so magnificent, so beautiful!
And you do change, as the stars shift in the sky,
so do your crags and cliffs move to an orchestration
like a cello, like an oboe, like a bass guitar!"

At this the mountain shifted again,
and jutted another avalanche of ice and snow,
down the walls of stone to the river below.
"But do you know, of time that goes and goes,
like the wrinkles on a nose,
carved into my sides, and had so much time,
that you cease to wonder why?"

She thought again, and pondered a frown.
Time passed for days, and on and on,
till she finally climbed down.

On her way back, to her village of suburbs,
she passed a river that ebbed,
and in it's calmly rippled reflections,
she saw the sky, and wondered why.

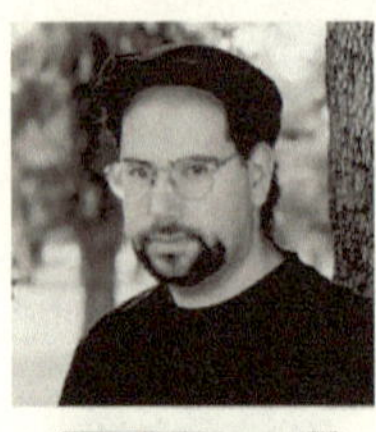

Donald R. Anderson, co-editor and co-publisher of *Sun Shadow Mountain,* has self-published chapbook anthologies and newsletters and websites. He has been in *!Zam Bomba!, Blue Moon Press, Rattlesnake Press,* and a small award in the contest by the Stockton Arts Commission a few years back for a poem titled *Suddenly a Fearsome Crow.* You contact him by emailing poetsespresso@yahoo.com or by visiting rainflowers.org online.

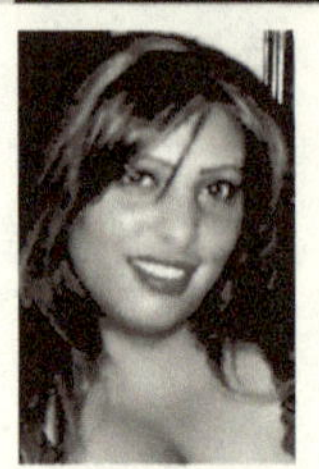

Nikki Quismondo is from Stockton, California. She is the co-editor and co-publisher of *Sun Shadow Mountain*, *Poet's Espresso* and *Midnight Dance/Pathos*, has been published in *Naked Poetry.* She was a featured poet at the Haggin Museum's *Elements of Poetry, 2005 Poetry Jam* in Stockton, California. She supports community events for local artists, and has judged the *2005 Poetry Contest* for *Barnes and Noble.* Email her at: pisces03142001@yahoo.com

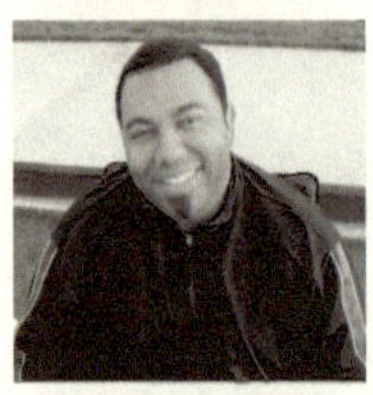

Lance Hudson is the copy editor of *Sun Shadow Mountain*. He was born in San Mateo, CA. He is a singer-songwriter, jazz-fusion guitarist, and poet. He has produced a screenplay entitled *The Trunk*. His band, *Human Anomaly,* has produced a 5-song recording entitled *Blind Juggler* on *Life Is Abuse Records*. Lance's solo project consists of 15 songs entitled *The Art of Solitude*. You may contact him at: anomaly@musician.org

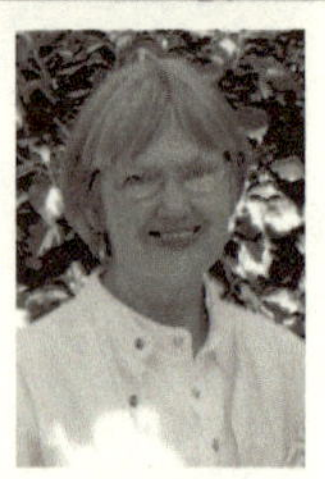

Patricia Wellingham-Jones, a former psychology researcher and writer/editor, is a three-time *Pushcart Prize* nominee. Chapbooks include *Don't Turn Away: Poems About Breast Cancer* (PWJ Publishing) and *Hormone Stew* (Snark Publishing). She won the *Palabra Productions Chapbook Contest* with *End-Cycle*, poems about care giving. Her website is www.wellinghamjones.com .

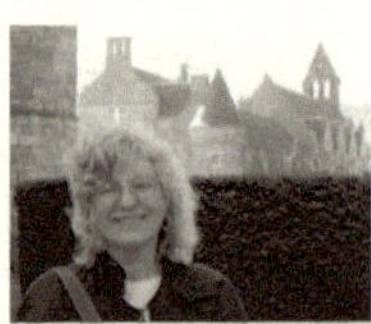

Jeanine Stevens has been published in *Tiger's Eye, Rattlesnake Review, Ruah, Timber Creek Review, Poetry Depth Quarterly, Sierra Nevada College Review*, and *Bardsong*. Besides writing, she enjoys Balkan folk dancing, traveling, and snowshoe and hiking jaunts in the Sierras. She was the first place adult poetry winner of the *10th Annual Writing Contest of the Stockton Arts Commission.*

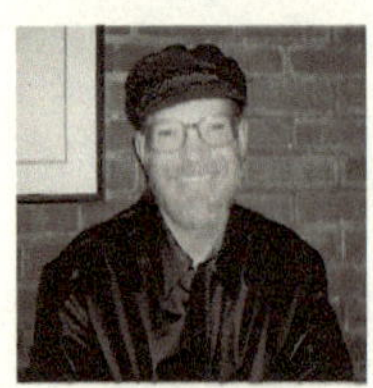

David Humphreys is a publisher who has written poetry for forty years. He founded *Poets Corner* as a radio broadcast, poetry reading series, audio/text website in 1997 located at www.poetscornerpress.com He has published over 25 books of poetry by other poets at *Poets Corner* Press since 2001. Five of his own books have been published including *My Shepherd* and *Our Father Who*, and he has collected over 70 publishing credits in magazines, journals, reviews, newspapers, online magazines.

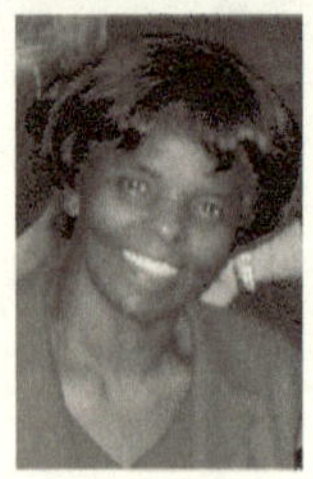

Mable "Jimi" Choice has been an educator and counselor for the Stockton Unified School District for over 40 years. She has been highly involved in serving groups such as "*Black Family Day, Dare Different Productions, NAACP ACT-SO, Academic, Cultural, Technological and Scientific Olympics programs, City and Statewide Black Student Union Programs*, classroom lectures, community poetry nights and theater events.

Tommy Dunn, who participated in the Art Students League of Staten Island, and has a B.A. from Staten Island, has always loved art. He's been doing it for years and thanks god for the creative inspiration that finds itself in all creative people.

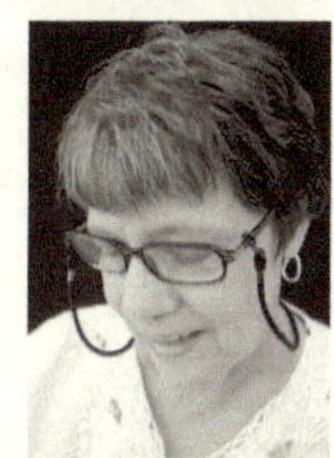

Marie J. Ross has read her poetry at open-mic-venues locally and in the central valley, and is a published poet, her poem *Oh Honored Stone* is inscribed at the *Veterans Memorial Plaza* in Lodi, California. She has a recently published book collaboration with Elizabeth Parrish titled *Lavender Fields*.

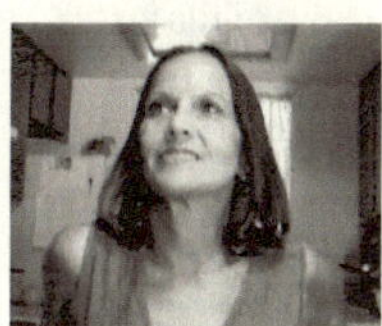

Lorrie Salvetti, from Stockton, CA, has done poetic, and inspirational writing since age 17. When her daughter was born, she became much more involved in her writing. She has been published in various central California newspapers, newsletters, and anthologies by groups such as *The American Poetry Association*, *The National Library of Poetry*, *The Amherst Society* and *Sparrowgrass*.

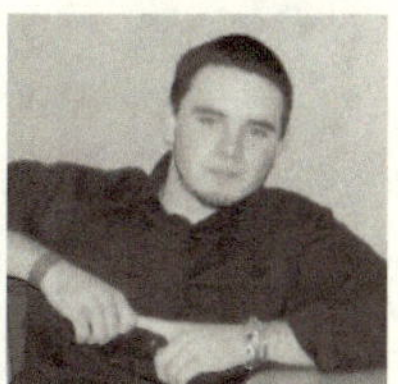

Charley Stockdale is an artist and poet in the Stockton, CA. who has generously submitted his art pieces to *Poet's Espresso*. He has been in art shows, published in *Midnight Dance/Pathos*, and is an active member of the poetry open mics. You may contact him at: ringsaroundeyes@hotmail.com.

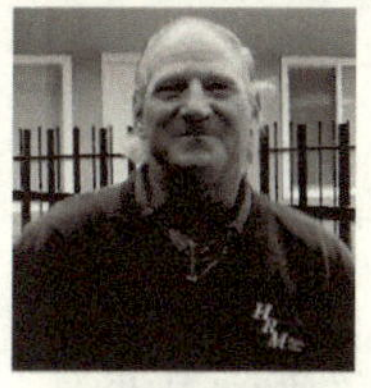

Wayne Robinson, married with children, is a work-a-holic bicycle rider, scuba diver, poetry writer. He loves life and people with a good attitude. Born 1952 in Oklahoma, living in California since 1956. A construction worker, who writes as often as possible. He has been known to bike long distances such as to Mount Diablo.

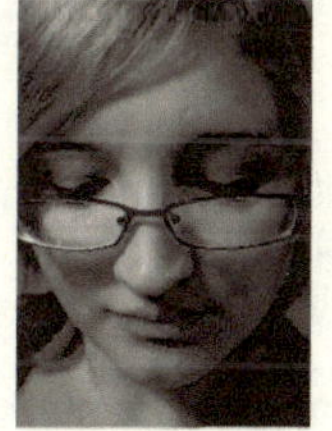

Reina Hutchison is a full time mom and full time student at San Joaquin Delta College in Stockton, CA. She is currently studying Photography and Journalism in hopes of making her two greatest passions a lifelong career. She is the editor the San Joaquin Delta College Writers' Guild publication *Artifact*. You may email her at gunner2s_grl@hotmail.com.

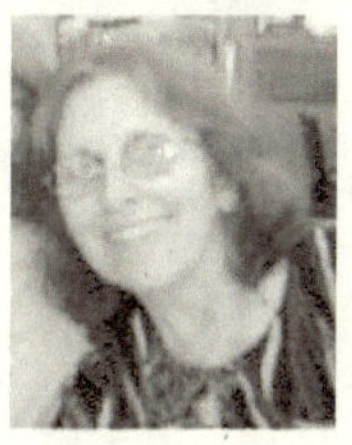

Ann Privateer's favorite personas are that of poet and photographer. She grew up in Cleveland, Ohio and now lives in northern California. Some of her poems have appeared in *Manzanita, Poetry and Prose of the Mother Lode and Sierra, The Arts of the Sierra & Sacramento Region, Tiger's Eye*, and *The Sacramento Anthology: One Hundred Poems*.

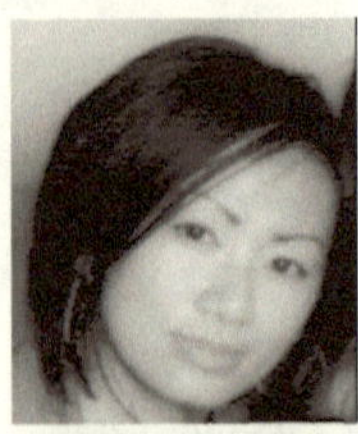

Chinetana (NA^2) Phounsavath was conceived by Somchith & Vilay Phounsavath, born in Laos, & full grown in Stockton, CA. She has extended her family tree by producing two "Seeds" of her own: Artatum & Asiel. Her work has been published in *Poet's Espresso* newsletter, one in *Liad's Literary Excellence*, and in *Artifact*. To preview her work, log on to: www.myspace.com/nasquared or wait for the complete poem book w/ accompanying CD, entitled *Silence Thoughts…w/ a Voice*.

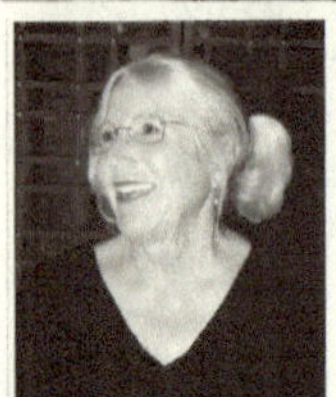

Marie Riepenhoff-Talty is from Roseville, CA. She has a PhD. in Microbiology from the State University of New York at Buffalo and spent the better part of thirty years studying the pathology and immunology of viruses. Before that she was a registered nurse. She has been writing poetry for a little over two years and has had poems published in *Rattlesnake Review*, *Poet's Forum Magazine* and *Medusa's Kitchen*.

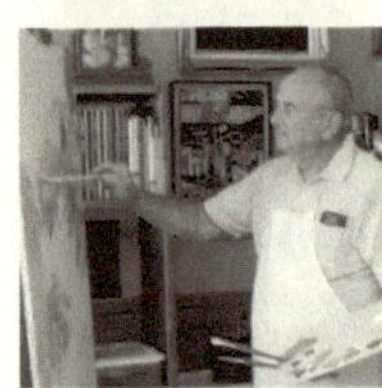

William Anderson began at an early age with some natural abilities in art. He spent most of his work years applying these abilities to commercial applications of art. He was able to find occupation in designing and pictorial work. There were some times that he ventured into fine arts and sold watercolors of the gold country at a gallery in Murphy's. There have been some shows that he has participated in through the years including a couple "one man shows". Now that he has "retired", he is devoting as much time as possible to the fine arts because it was something he has always wanted to do.

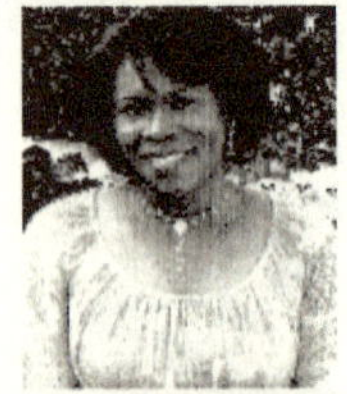

Shonda Renée is the host of *Poets On The Roof* , the Stockton Poet's Workshop, which you can visit at www.poetsontheroof.com. She has published a chapbook collection of her poetry entitled *Bearings* in 2003.

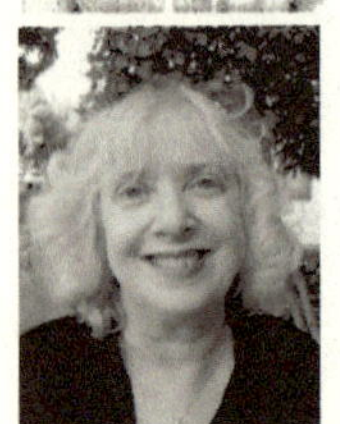

Elizabeth Parrish was born in Cambridge, Massachusetts. She delved into poetry at an early age. She graduated from San Francisco State University with a B.A. in English. She has taught English and creative writing. She edits a newsletter for the American Association of University Women and reads at various venues in Stockton. She has a recently published book collaboration with Marie J. Ross titled *Lavender Fields*.

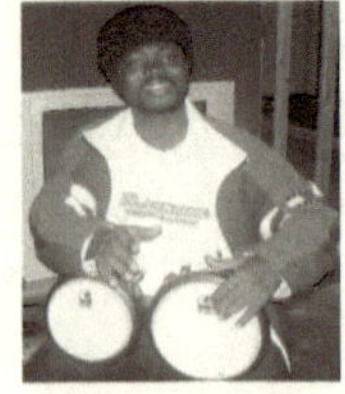

Jean Claude Crhi was born in Cameroun in Africa. He has traveled and studied in many places, including Europe and the United States, where he now lives. Jean Claude Crhi is an author of children's books, such as *The Queen and Mrs. Earth*. He is an artist, musician and humanitarian. Jean Claude has been in active member in supporting artists and poets and has hosted many poetry events in the San Joaquin Valley and Bay Area of California.

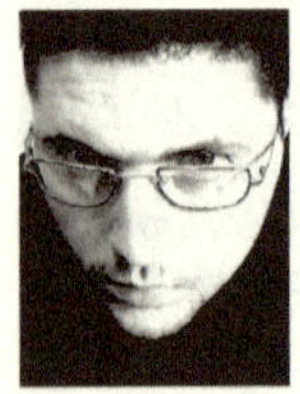

Tony Melrose is a science fiction/fantasy artist who works mostly in black and white but has also created several color pieces. Tony was born and raised just outside Dallas Texas.

Jeff Giampetro has been a computer artist for 10 years now. He studied at the *Academy of Art College* in San Francisco and does all different types of media graphics, film, photography.

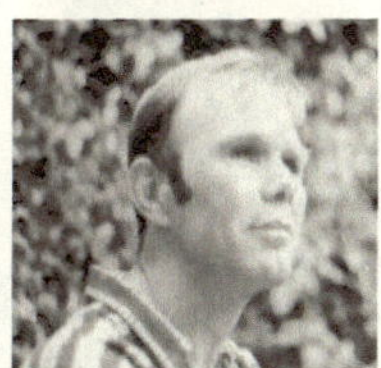

Joe Tetro resides in Bakersfield, California. After a rural childhood, the military, and getting a B.A. in German, Joe moved to Mexico at age 65 and wrote poems on scraps of used lumber about"*...herring-gutted village dogs abandoning the gravesides of dusty memories*," and "*... wine weeping into the lap of the ocean's ruffled skirts.*" At 95 he'll be writing about the rise and the fall of the American Empire. He can be contacted at: joe.tetro@yahoo.com.

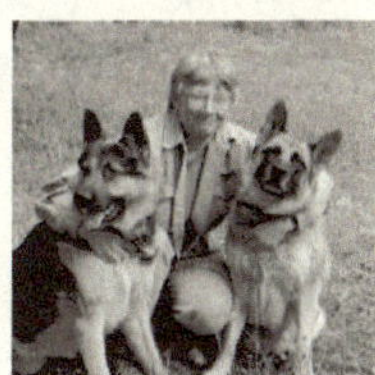

Taylor Graham is a volunteer search-and-rescue dog handler in El Dorado County, and also help her husband (a retired wildlife biologist) with his field projects. Taylor Graham is included in the anthology, *California Poetry: From the Gold Rush to the Present*, and her latest book, *The Downstairs Dance Floor*, is winner of the *Robert Phillips Poetry Chapbook Prize*.

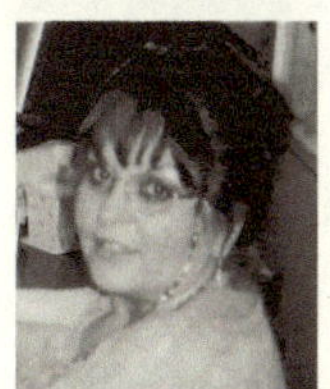

Patricia Mayorga, from Stockton, CA, is an educator and program specialist for Stockton Unified School District. Patricia is a published poetess whose poetry has been published in a collection entitled *Days of Thirst* as well as in the National Library of Congress anthologies, *Beyond The Stars* and *A Tapestry of Thoughts*. Her poetry has also been published in local publications such as *Poet's Espresso* and *!Zam Bomba!*. Patricia and her husband reside in Stockton.

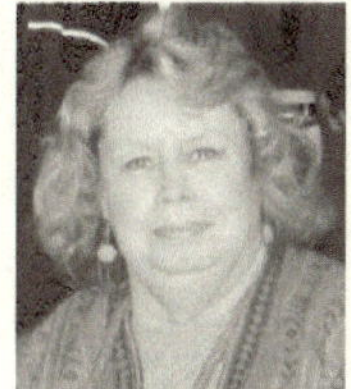

Gail Lee White is a native Californian from Napa, who loves nature, words, and color. She has been published in the anthologies *Naked Poetry* and *Midnight Dance/Pathos.*

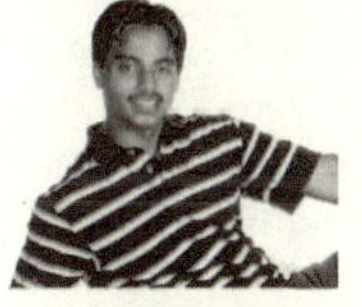

Joseph Aaron Quismondo Hernandez is a high school student at the *Benjamin Holt College Preparatory Academy.* He is an athlete rower for the *Delta Blades* rowing team and is and artist and poet.

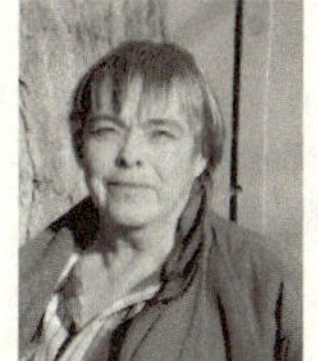

Stephani Schaefer is a recent transplant to NorCal from New Mexico's high desert (thus her experience with the games mountains play out there). She has had work in *Hembra, Conceptions SW, the rag, Krax, Rattlesnake Review*, on *Dial-a-Poem* and on *Medusa's Kitchen*.

Marjorie Wagler Carmack lives in Modesto, California. Her poems were published in a compilation called, *World Treasury of Golden Poems*, 1990.

Andy Pope, currently a Lodi resident, is a lifelong musician, writer, and theatre person. An avid long-distance runner, he is a member of the Episcopal Church of Saint John the Baptist. His writings tend to express religious themes in ways that are unique and unusual. He is most recently the author-composer of a musical play entitled *The Burden of Eden*.

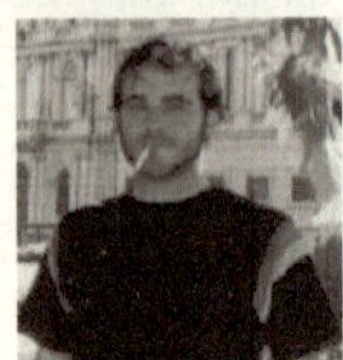

Stephen M. Wilson, Poetry Editor for Doorways Magazine (www.doorwaysmag.com), has work nominated for five *Rhyslings*, a *Dwarf Stars Award*, and a *John B. Baker Award*, garnered an Honorable Mention in *Year's Best Fantasy and Horror 2006* and was a finalist for L. Ron Hubbard's *Writers of the Future Award*. Upcoming publications include: *HUNGUR, STAR*LINE, SCIFAIKUEST, THE MAGAZINE OF SPECULATIVE POETRY, RAW MEAT, and THE VAULT OF PUNK HORROR*.

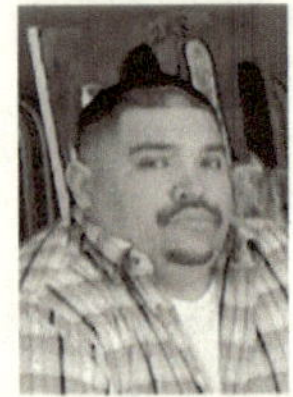

Sergio Navarro lives in Stockton, California. He has been painting for 7 years and writing poetry for 10 years. His art works have been featured in Stockton, California's *Art Walk* in 2006 and in *Barnes and Noble* in February of 2007.

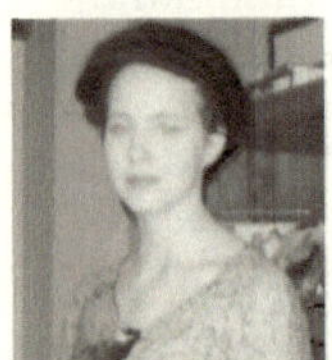

Raederle Phoenix An Lydell West lives in Buffalo, New York. She is an artist, poet, writer. Her poetry online can be found at http://poeticdragon.diaryland.com, and her art at http://button-maker.diaryland.com.

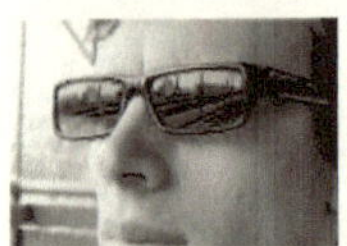

Josh Hutchison is from Lodi, California. He plans on starting metal sculpture. He stops time with a shutter. He knows that his images are only half truths, a whole story cannot be told by a picture. His page is at www.myspace.com/joshgunner.

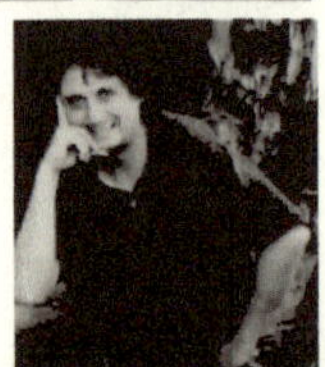

Jim Ricks has been featured in *!Zam Bomba!* and *Status Unknown*. He is also an accomplished pianist.

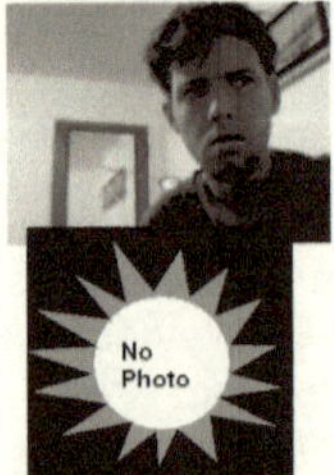

Stephen Cothran started writing poetry when he was 15 and kept to it. He is a San Joaquin Delta College student.

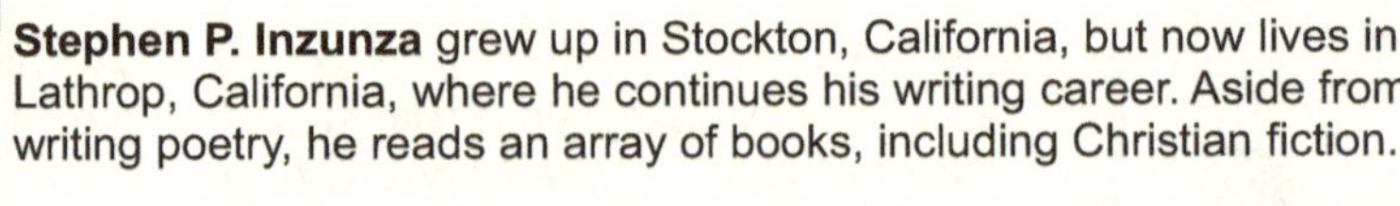

Stephen P. Inzunza grew up in Stockton, California, but now lives in Lathrop, California, where he continues his writing career. Aside from writing poetry, he reads an array of books, including Christian fiction.

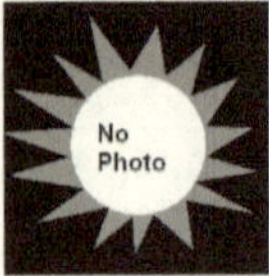

Pedro Colon, also known as Mambo, lives in New York city and is a retired musician. He teaches martial arts is from the island of Puerto Rico.

www.ingramcontent.com/pod-product-compliance
Lightning Source LLC
LaVergne TN
LVHW090951080826
845145LV00003B/965

* 9 7 8 0 6 1 5 1 4 7 6 0 4 *

"*Seeing Is Believing* breaks new ground for Christians desiring to become more discerning filmgoers. Helping viewers move beyond mere plot analysis, Goodwin heightens our awareness of what images also accomplish. If you love going to movies, you'll love reading this book. You'll also love watching your next movie more!"

Robert K. Johnston, senior professor of theology and culture and codirector of Brehm Film at Fuller Theological Seminary

"Protestant theology has never known quite what to do with visual images of any kind, much less moving images. In *Seeing Is Believing,* Richard Goodwin short-circuits the ambivalence toward the visual that has long defined (Protestant) theological engagements with film. In doing so, he doesn't merely invite us to clarify our vision with respect to the theological significance of film. Rather, as if we were Neo emerging from the Matrix, Goodwin asks us to consider what might transpire if we actually used our eyes, perhaps for the very first time."

Kutter Callaway, associate professor of theology and culture at Fuller Theological Seminary and author of *Deep Focus: Film and Theology in Dialogue*

"Lucidly summarizing multiple ways theologians through the ages have understood God's revelation, Richard Vance Goodwin suggests that cinema can be a source of revelatory power for those with eyes to see. Seeing, in fact, is key to his approach as he discusses the way visual techniques in four classic films mediate divine content. Astutely arguing against the reduction of film to a vehicle for either Christian messages or transcendent experiences, Goodwin gives a refreshingly new and thoroughly Christian spin to reception studies and cognitivism in film theory."

Crystal L. Downing, author of *Salvation from Cinema: The Medium is the Message*

"Finally! A theological discussion of cinema that focuses on and takes pleasure in *how* a cinematic story is told, not merely in what the story supposedly means. Goodwin's book leads students of theology and film in the right direction, away from easy moralizing and toward a more enthusiastic encounter with God's active presence in the light that reflects off the silver screen."

Elijah Davidson, author of *How to Talk to a Movie: Movie-Watching as a Spiritual Exercise* and codirector of the Brehm Film Institute at Fuller Theological Seminary

"A number of books in recent years have studied film as a medium of theological exploration and insight, but most have focused on the story line that particular films develop. In this book, Richard Goodwin breaks new ground by exploring the ways in which the cinematographic techniques and devices through which the story is conveyed may themselves become instruments of divine revelation. In so doing, this book opens up a rich new avenue of exploration in the field of theology and film. I am glad to commend it to scholars and film lovers alike."

Murray Rae, University of Otago in Dunedin, New Zealand

"Seeking to illumine the revelatory way in which God may affectively reveal Godself in cinema, Goodwin assesses transcendence—sparse or abundant—and emotion through film form and style: image, lighting, mise en scène, and editing. This book is an important read for filmmakers of faith, for it illuminates both aesthetic and potent means of inhabiting God's presence and story through cinema without words."

Rebecca Ver Straten-McSparran, film consultant, theologian, and author of *Lars von Trier's Cinema: Excess, Evil, and the Prophetic Voice*